GW01185642

SCENIC
SOUTH AFRICA

AUGUST SYCHOLT
PETER SCHIRMER

STRUIK

Struik Publishers (Pty) Ltd
(a member of The Struik Publishing Group (Pty) Ltd)
Cornelis Struik House
80 McKenzie Street
Cape Town 8001

Reg. No. 54/00965/07

First published as *This is South Africa* in 1981
First published in softcover in 1985
Second impression 1988
Third impression 1989
Fourth impression 1990
Fifth impression 1992
First published as *Scenic South Africa* in 1994

Text © The Struik Publishing Group (Pty) Ltd 1981, 1985, 1994
Photographs © August Sycholt 1981, 1985, 1994 with the exception of:
Cloete Breytenbach: 259, 279;
N Dennis: back cover (bottom);
Doreen Hemp: 8, 154;
Walter Knirr: cover and cover insets (top left, bottom right, centre), 6, 7,
29, 153, 157, 242, 243;
Peter Pickford: 240;
Herman Potgieter: 14, 45, 168, 190, 191, 193, 195, 216, 269, 274, 278, 281;
David Steele: 185;
Struik Image Library: cover inset (top right) [L Hoffmann], cover inset
(bottom left) [E Thiel], cover inset (top right) title page, back cover (top)
[P Pickford];
Sun International 291, 292, 293, 294.

All rights reserved. No part of this publication may be reproduced,
stored in a retrieval system, or transmitted, in any form or by any means,
electronic, mechanical, photocopying, recording or otherwise, without
the prior written permission of the copyright owner(s).

Editor (1994 edition): Brenda Brickman
Cover design by Lyndall Hamilton
Designer: Neville Poulter

Photoset by Unifoto (Pty) Ltd, Cape Town
Reproduction by Tien Wah Press (Pte) Ltd, Singapore
Printing and binding by Kyodo Printing Co. (Pte) Ltd, Singapore

ISBN 1-86825-609-X

The graceful proportions of a gabled Cape Dutch homestead (frontispiece) are an ever-present link between the history of the western Cape and its agricultural present – a gentle scene in striking contrast to the stark majesty of the Drakensberg (title page). Both though are as integral a part of South Africa as a young Xhosa initiate (**3**) or a thundering lorry traversing the landscape near Newcastle (**4**) where ox-wagons once rolled across the veld.

SCENIC SOUTH AFRICA

His stumpy legs were so short and weak that they could move his grotesque body only when the mud and ooze of the primeval swamp helped bear his mass. His tremendously thick cranium contained a minute brain, and though scientists were to call him a 'fearsome head', he was an inoffensive herbivore who existed on a diet of ferns and cycads. He was *Tapinocephalus,* and about 200 million years ago he slurched through the vast, steaming swamps of Gondwanaland where today the semi-desert of South Africa's Karoo bakes aridly in the sun.

Save as fossils, nothing of his world remains except the cycads, which still flourish in several parts of the Republic and are unique to her flora. The swamp he inhabited was compressed and changed as ice ages came and receded. Tremendous geomorphic forces deep within the earth's core rent Gondwanaland to form, among others, South America, South Africa and Australasia. And these same forces spewed forth the volcanic pipes which were to give the Republic her diamond riches, while others laid down a vast sedimentary saucer of gold whose rim is mined today to provide the backbone of South Africa's economy.

Tapinocephalus is remembered only by scientists, and his ancient presence commemorated by a reconstruction in the South African Museum in Cape Town. But, as one of the first mammal-like reptiles, he was an important link in the evolutionary chain which was to provide the subcontinent with the unsurpassed range of animal life found here today. And though the vast herds of game that once teemed across the country are no more – scattered and compressed by the advent of man – their descendants are to be seen, sometimes in the few

△3

wild spaces that remain, more frequently in the country's numerous game parks dedicated to their preservation.

Their predecessors knew no such sanctuaries. Excavations have revealed that the early man-apes – found at Taung and 900 000 years older than Neanderthal man – were effective prototypes for Man the Predator. Scientists have also discovered that the Stone-Age peoples who inhabited much of the subcontinent 25 000 years ago, possessed relatively refined hunting techniques. Their hunter-gatherer existence was, in fact, little different to that of the Bushmen who for millennia shared the 1 134 100 km² that is South Africa with fauna which they killed for food or in self-defence. Pockets of these little people, whose social structure based on sharing would be the envy of both Christ and Karl Marx, still exist. But rock-paintings in the shelters they inhabited, show that once they roamed the whole wide land from the sparkling coastal beaches to the rugged inland ranges, and from the lush subtropical forests of the east to the timeless deserts of the west where the remnants of their people still maintain something of their ancient life-style.

They knew of the underground honeycomb that is the Cango Caves, but lacked powerful light to explore the natural gallery of its stalactites and stalagmites which spotlights now reveal – a wonderland for today's visitor. Some of these early Bushmen may have paused beside a sapling yellowwood in the Knysna Forest, neither thinking nor caring that 1 700 years later the modern tourist would crane his neck in an attempt to see its tip towering 42 m above the ground, or marvel as he paced its 8-m girth. Certainly they themselves marvelled at the force of the Orange River as it thundered over its series of cascades, for they gave the Aughrabies Falls its name 'the great waters', which the Korana tribes corrupted to auKarabis and we, in turn, corrupted to its present form.

But the Bushmen were gradually driven from the land. Black

tribes arrived from the north, moving ever south and westwards with the herds of cattle that were their wealth. Much later white settlers – sent to the Cape to establish a victualling post for the ships of the Dutch East India Company en route to gather the riches of the Orient – expanded outwards to the north and east. Both were foreign to the land; both were to leave an indelible stamp on it – and continue to do so. Both were to multiply here, so that today nearly 40 million people inhabit the country – about eight times as many as at the turn of the century. The black African population stands at over 30 million; the white at just under 5 million (compared with the less than 100 that comprised the first colonial settlement); the Afro-European and Indian at something over 4 million. The population as a whole is expanding at a rapid, even alarming rate.

The meeting of black and white and the clash of their disparate cultures was traumatic, leading to bloodshed which was to continue for centuries. But confrontation was not new to this part of Africa. Tribesmen were already killing tribesmen in a series of conflicts that were to reach charnel-house proportions with Shaka's forging of the mighty Zulu nation and the *Difaqane,* or forced migrations, which accompanied his expansionist reign.

And it was the white colonists' need to expand that led to the protracted series of Frontier wars, spanning more than a century, in which first the Dutch and then the British were to clash with the Xhosa tribes. These people, never defeated in battle, were brought down by the predictions of a young prophetess whose visions persuaded them to destroy their crops and to kill their cattle.

It was to act as a buffer between the established settlements of the western Cape and the black tribes that the 1820 Settlers were brought from Britain – to leave a greater English imprint on the country than that of any colonial administration. And it was to escape the ongoing conflict and the rigidity of laws

which stemmed from it, that the Boer farmers were to venture inland on their Great Trek, opening up the hinterland for the eventual discovery of gold and diamonds, the first pointers to South Africa's vast mineral treasure-house.

These stubborn pioneers were the first to counter the might of the Zulu armies. Their epic journey and the greatest clash between black and white is commemorated in the Voortrekker Monument on a koppie outside Pretoria. Surrounded by an imitation bas-relief of 60 laagered ox-waggons in a protective circle around its base, it remains to many Afrikaners the most important tangible symbol of their nationhood. For them it is a symbol not only of physical but of spiritual significance. Through a specially placed aperture in the monument's roof, precisely at noon on December 16 each year, the rays of the sun strike through the vaulted ceiling to touch the centre of the cenotaph beneath . . . on the day most spiritually significant in the calendar of many Afrikaners. It was on this day in 1838 that

a small but well-armed force of Trekkers defeated the Zulu armies ... 100 years later the foundation stones of the monument were laid ... and in 1949 it was officially opened.

But the land had not seen the last of bloodshed, for white was to clash with white in the pain and horror of two wars, as the two small Boer republics withstood the might of the British Empire to defend their political beliefs, even as the shields and *assegais* of the Zulus had withstood the firepower of the whites to defend their land and their cultures.

The uneasy truce that followed the Anglo-Boer War led to the creation of the modern South African state. But the clash of cultures persisted throughout the eight decades following Union, and it was only in 1994 that South Africa's leaders finally managed to fashion the blueprint for a wholly nonracial society – and in doing so set the country on a course to becoming a shining model for other troubled communities, both within and beyond the continent of Africa.

5△   7▽

Starkly etched skyscrapers and the needle of the Post Office tower throw Johannesburg's skyline into sharp relief against the dying reds and golds of a typical highveld sunset (5). A mining camp scarcely a century ago, today the third largest city on the African continent retains a youthful brashness which the mature elements – the encircling freeways, futuristic blocks of offices and other modern developments – cannot conceal.

The streets of the central area are long and narrow, for when gold was first found here the Transvaal republican authorities reacted cautiously to the news, believing that the seam was a modest one, and that the mines would be short-lived. Johan Rissik, the Government Surveyor, set aside a waterless expanse of bushveld terrain and instructed the planners to lay out a town in close grid – in order to create the maximim number of corner plots. These were considered

▽8   6△

more valuable and thus greater spinners of revenue for the coffers of Paul Kruger's young republic. In the event, the first of them was sold on December 10, 1886 for half-a-crown, others for a mere 30 shillings – less than a barrel of drinking water fetched at that time.

Today Johannesburg is the country's premier city, a bustling, cosmopolitan metropolis girded by dense rings of satellite towns huddling in an area known as the Witwatersrand and which, collectively, generates around half South Africa's national income. Despite its youth and its rugged, no-nonsense materialism, though, the place has real claims to sophistication,

even stylishness. The shopping malls rival the best in the world; fine cuisine is offered by a myriad restaurants; the social scene is exuberant; the visual and performing arts thrive. Among the more prominent venues is the Market

Theatre (8), a four-auditorium complex that caters for tastes ranging from local and experimental drama to drawing-room comedy. The building, which once functioned as the Indian fruit and citrus market, also encloses a shopping arcade, art gallery, restaurant, bistro and jazz bar. The theatre fronts onto Fitzgerald Square, which hosts one of the city's bigger and busier flea markets (6). Central Johannesburg doesn't offer a great deal of greenery – space is in short supply and nearly all of it has been filled by high-rise concrete and glass – but the suburbs are graced by some 600 parks and open spaces, among them charming Emmarentia Dam (7).

Where the streets of other early Transvaal towns were planned wide enough for an ox-waggon and its team to turn in, those of central Johannesburg – lined on each side by parked vehicles – would make such a manoeuvre impossible, even for the smallest modern car. And in the rush-hour drivers may well envy the oxen's speed as traffic travels through the Hillbrow dusk (9) leaving the business centre almost deserted as the daily motorcades of commuters return to the suburbs. In Hillbrow's high-walled arteries, the human pulse of the city beats for 24 hours of every day and the strum of a street musician's guitar (10) is as likely to be heard at midnight as at noon.

11△ 12▽ 13▽

But it is for its business pulse that Johannesburg is internationally renowned. Its modern stock exchange – whose glass-sided lifts (12) provide a pigeon's-eye view of what was once the Ferreira's town camp (infant Johannesburg was divided into four separate areas, each of which is now an inner suburb) – has one of the busiest trading floors of any of the world's bourses. Though it was not the first stock exchange in South Africa – in the heyday of the De Kaap Valley diggings of the Eastern Transvaal, just before the discovery of the Witwatersrand fields in 1886, the Barberton camp boasted two exchanges – it was the only one to have lasted, coming a long way from the early days when miners and speculators exchanged scrip 'between the chains' – literally old wagon chains strung from posts on a piece of barren veld.

While still the 'city of gold' in the world's imagination, or *eGoli* – literally 'gold' – to South Africa's 30 million blacks, in economic terms Johannesburg today is the centre of the Republic's industrial heartland – the Witwatersrand-Pretoria-Vereeniging complex – whose factories produce a kaleidoscopic range of products, rivalled by the Aladdin's Cave of international wares available in the city's shops. In malls and arcades such as the rotunda beneath the Carlton Centre (11), Japanese transistor radios, leather goods from Italy, German cameras and *haute couture* Parisienne silks reveal the Johannesburger's materialistic progress, symbols of the hustler city's success. The towering 51-storey Carlton Centre is regarded with pride by most of *eGoli*'s inhabitants as the true 'symbol of modern Johannesburg.' The complex is dominated by a 222-metre-tall tower block which is the world's largest reinforced concrete building – and a far cry from the tents and corrugated-iron shacks which spawned South Africa's biggest and most modern city.

14△ 15▽

The vast web of Soweto (**14**), the 'city within a city', is the home of an estimated three million people. Every day from this urban sprawl which crouches on Johannesburg's south-western flank, the hundreds of thousands who comprise its main labour force teem into *eGoli* and the factories of Johannesburg's periphery. Soweto earned international notoriety from political protests which sometimes erupted into violence, a violence belying the precise network of its streets and the dull repetitiveness of its housing.

As in any city, Soweto is the home of millionaires and paupers, of saints and sinners; but social lines, demarcated by wealth or occupation, are less rigid. Des-

16△   17▽

pite the growth of black urban society, in which traditional customs are falling away, tribal groupings remain important. Even the gangs of street children (**15**), who huddle round street-corner fires, tend to form according to tribal groupings. Many of them exist on the pickings of petty crime in a ragamuffin existence which precludes the formal education others enjoy (**17**). And though, in theory at least, any of these youths or children could become doctors or lawyers – the professions which remain the 'plums' of black aspirations – a scarcity of classroom space, coupled with a dearth of teachers and ongoing boycotts, has limited the attainment of higher educa-

tion to relatively few. Official efforts to improve black educational facilities must struggle against the realities of limited funds and an exploding birthrate.

This 'explosion' promises that before the turn of the century Soweto's population will have surpassed that of its 'parent'. Presently part of Johannesburg, rapid progress is being made towards its autonomy and independent municipal status. Already a myriad entrepreneurs have set up small businesses and the mini-city boasts several commercial and shopping complexes. For their more sophisticated or expensive purchases, however, most residents prefer the hypermarkets and departmental stores of central Johannesburg.

There the choice is greater, the prices more competitive and the increasing purchasing power of a rapidly growing black middle-class is recognized and catered for.

If the week is given over to work and Saturday mornings to shopping, the balance of Soweto's weekend reverberates to the enthusiasm of sport, of which soccer is the uncrowned king (**16**). Among most South African blacks, soccer is as much of a cult as rugby is among the majority of whites. And it was in such soccer stadiums as those of Soweto that the first multiracial sides were fielded – breaching the now-dismantled apartheid system and setting the lead for other athletic spheres.

◁
18

19△   20▽

The detribalization of the urban black has created a new society with its own values and culture, but some spheres remain where tradition and custom still fight a largely succesful rearguard action. Thus, whether in the rural ambience of the kraal, or the city slickness of the townships, the diviner continues to play a role which has changed little for several centuries. A mixture of soothsayer and psychologist, it is the diviner – often mistakenly labelled a witch-doctor – who intercedes with the spirit of the ancestors and acts as the channel through which the wishes or advice of his forebears are conveyed to the supplicant.

Diviners (**18**) are the readers of signs and throwers of bones, often ostentatiously displaying the trappings of their trade and decorating the walls of their establishments with colourful symbols (**19**)

which are an eye-catching mixture of signs representative of both pagan and western beliefs. Recruited to their calling by the ancestors for whom they act as terrestrial go-betweens, the diviners usually undergo a rigorous apprenticeship before beginning to practise their art. Methods differ from tribe to tribe, but the 'ailments' which they treat are generally the result of social or spiritual stress, frequently psychosomatic, and heightened for many newcomers to the townships by the conflict between tribal and western culture.

One of South Africa's best-known witch-doctors, Credo Mutwa (**20**), caused a furore amongst his peers when he pub-

21▽

lished two books *Ndaba my children* and *Africa is my witness* which purported to reveal the history of southern Africa's blacks and their medical and spiritual 'secrets'. Despite the scorn with which many greeted his revelations, Mutwa continues to enjoy a thriving practice.

Where the diviner's skills are mainly psychological, his counterpart the herbalist provides *muti,* or medicine, in the form of pills, powders, philtres and potions – and even charms or amulets. Modern research has proved that the bases of many of these medicines are pharmaceutically sound. Herbalists' shops (**21**) abound, their custom often drawn from whites as well as blacks.

22△ 23▽

South Africa, though generously endowed with many other minerals, is synonymous with gold; and the mine dumps – titanic refuse heaps of crushed reef from which the precious metal has been extracted – are a constant reminder of the Midas riches which lie beneath the Highveld's landscape. From the region has come 40% of all the world's gold in the past century. The goldfields lie in a great 500 km arc from Evander in the northeast to Virginia in the south, on what geologists believe to be the rim of a giant, gold saucer laid down some 2 700 million years ago and since covered by deposits of sedimentary and volcanic rock.

Even with today's sophisticated tech-

△24

25▽

niques, more than three tonnes of rock have to be crushed for every ounce of gold recovered, and the older dumps, such as this one at Maraisburg (**22**), bear silent testimony to the back-breaking efforts of the first miners. Something of the problems with which they had to contend, and their often primitive equipment, can be gleaned from this old steam locomotive (**24**), an active work-horse and a tourist attraction at one of Johannesburg's older mines.

The simplicity of the early methods of recovery, coupled with the rising price of the metal, has provided a bonus for modern technology. Since 1978, residual gold has been recovered from the che-

mical recycling of old dumps and slimes dams. But the bulk of the 600 tonnes of gold which South African mines produce each year, and which comprises well over a quarter of the world's output is re-covered far beneath the surface. From narrow stopes, often little more than a metre high, the ore-bearing rock and the

men who mine it are hauled upwards by special lifts, their presence marked by the headgear such as this (**23**) on an old mine south of Johannesburg. Brought to the surface, the rock is washed, sorted and crushed before being ground into 'fines' which then undergo a complex chemical process to extract the precious metal. It is then smelted and poured to form the 31,1 kg gold ingots containing some 83% gold and 9% silver, which are further refined at a central plant in Germiston. Even there, these gold-green bricks do not reach absolute purity, but a fineness of 996 parts in 1 000. This special ingot (**25**) is on public display at the Chamber of Mines in Johannesburg.

26△ 27▽
▷28

A molten stream of gold cascades into a form (**26**) at West Driefontein, the world's richest mine which has yielded 1 470 000 kg of gold since operations began here in 1945. A deep level mine, from which more than 17 tonnes of water have to be pumped for every tonne of ore-bearing rock recovered, Driefontein's workings plunge two kilometres below the surface. At these depths, despite refrigerated air being pumped through the honeycomb of tunnels, temperatures of 32°C are common, and humidity often reaches saturation.

Deeper into the earth's crust – at Western Deep Levels gold is being recovered 3,6 km underground – temperatures are correspondingly higher, reaching 60°C at the actual work-face. This intense heat, combined with the unstable nature of the rock through which the stopes are driven, create discomfort and hazards which continuing research attempts to alleviate. Sophisticated machinery has been developed and new techniques employed as a result of this research process; but in the

shallow stopes, working in Stygian darkness broken only by the comforting gleam of this headlamp (**27**), it is still the man, the miner, who must pit his paltry strength against Nature's subterranean forces – forces which can suddenly erupt causing injury and even death. But intensive safety precautions and elaborate techniques which warn of potential dangers have greatly reduced the risks of deep-level mining.

None of the 19th-century geologists suspected the presence of this golden treasure house, in spite of the rich finds of the Transvaal lowveld, and its discovery in 1886 by two itinerant diggers, was by sheer chance. George Harrison and George Walker were working as casual labourers on the farm 'Langlaagte' when, in search of suitable stone for the house they were building, they found the rock contained traces of gold. The pair had stumbled on the Witwatersrand's fabulous Main Reef (though neither

benefited: Harrison sold his claim for just £10!), and within three years of the discovery the mining camp of Johannesburg had mushroomed into the country's largest town.

Visitors have a number of sightseeing options, among them underground tours of a working concern (**28**) arranged through the Chamber of Mines. More evocative of the early days is Gold Reef City (**29**), a marvellously authentic re-creation of pioneer Johannesburg built on the historic Crown Mines site. Here one can explore the old workings (which yielded an impressive 1,4 kg of the yellow metal during their lifetime), observe gold being poured, and watch African traditional and 'gumboot' dancing. Among many other attractions are trips by steam train and horse-drawn omnibus; house museums furnished in period style; a Victorian funfair; replicas of an early pub, brewery, newspaper office, stock exchange, apothecary, cooperage and tailor's shop; and a variety of speciality stores.

30△ 31▽

▷ 32

Visitors in the early 1800s to the royal kraal of Shaka's Zulu empire wrote of the earth 'trembling' beneath the stamping feet of his *impis*, or regiments, as they executed the elaborate steps of rigidly-disciplined dances. Among all the black tribes of southern Africa, the innate sense of rhythm of their peoples found impressive expression in dance and song, whether it was ritual, narrative or recreational. The tradition has continued and when people – drawn from every tribe of the subcontinent – moved to the mines of the Witwatersrand, they brought their dances with them.

Such music as accompanies the dancers is provided by the often repetitive percussive hand-claps or chanting of the audience. Many Swazi dances are punctuated by the shrill whistle of the leader of each troupe (**30**) while others such as the amaZulu-ndlamu (**33**) beat a strict tempo with kerries on the small cowhide shields which they carry. In these all-male dances it is the leader who determines the routine not only of

33

the movements but also of the characteristic high kick followed by stamping in unison – the *indlamu* in which the ground literally shakes, and which is traditional only to the Bantu-speaking tribes of southern Africa. Among the Sotho, their blankets and conical straw hats contrasting sharply with their western trousers (**32**), this stamping is accompanied by the vast strides of the *mohobelo*.

Dancing often begins spontaneously, even among miners coming 'off-shift' at the end of a day spent underground. The spectacular 'gumboot dance' exemplifies this. Tribal finery (**31**) of shields, necklets and resplendent ostrich-plumes is, in fact, reserved for the organized dances.

34△ **35**▽

Where many of the Transvaal mine-workers and urban poor find their week-end recreation in soccer and in dance, their more affluent fellow citizens swarm to man-made and natural pleasure resorts – often several hours' drive away. Among the most popular of these, and almost equidistant from both Johannes-burg and Pretoria, is the Hartebeespoort Dam (**34**). Fed by the Crocodile and Magalies rivers, the dam was one of the first built in the Transvaal. Its wall has been heightened several times so that when full it covers 1 620 ha and sustains 15 000 ha of intensively cultivated land.

But agriculture is far from the minds of the weekend pleasure-seekers who throng its banks. Anglers young and old try to tempt the bass and carp with which its waters are stocked. Others enjoy the more active sailing and water-skiing for which there are abundant facilities. And ever along the shoreline drifts the tang of a hundred *braaivleis* fires.

At the weekend, throughout middle-class South Africa, the cult of the *braaivleis* reigns supreme (**36**). From patches of open veld to the manicured gardens of mansions and small suburban back-yards, the woodsmoke rises, bearing the aroma of grilling chops, steaks and *boerewors*, literally 'farmer's sausage'. And, as with any other cult, there are numerous schisms –

almost every suburban South African male (for 'braaing' is a man's work) is the ardent acolyte of the merits of the particular wood, or temperature, or spice best suited to his sacrifice. And – at least among the Afrikaners of the Transvaal – no *braai* is complete without an accompanying dish of *pap*, highly-spiced mealie-meal porridge prepared in three-legged cooking pots, of which the womenfolk are the cult's handmaidens (**35**).

Here too, the merits of recipes are argued hard and long. Indeed, the cult of the *braai* generates enough heated exchanges to fill a hot-air balloon on numerous crossings of another popular pleasure area – the Magaliesberg (**37**) ●

38△ 39▽ 41▽

40▽

Where Johannesburg is brashly and busily dedicated to finance and commerce, Pretoria is more sedate, its even pace fitted to that of the thousands of civil servants and scores of diplomats for whom – for much of each year at least – this city is home. Pretoria is the country's administrative capital – dedicated to the business of government. Surrounded by hills over which its residential suburbs and administrative buildings have gradually crawled, the city is also the home of the world's largest university teaching exclusively by correspondence. From its starkly-modern headquarters on Muckleneuk Ridge (38),

43 △ 44 ▽

◁ 42

each year the University of South Africa provides courses for more than 60 000 students of all races drawn from the entire sub-continent.

But it is the Union Buildings (42) which dominate Pretoria. From their imposing site on Meintjieskop they are visible from every corner of the city. Designed by Sir Herbert Baker and largely in the renaissance tradition, the two main sections, linked by Grecian colonnades, surround an amphitheatre from whose central steps the equestrian statue of General Louis Botha, first prime minister of a united South Africa, surveys a swathe of landscaped gardens.

While the Union Buildings are the embodiment of Pretoria, Church Square (39, 40, 41) remains its heart. Tranquil now and rimmed by buildings of both old and new, it was here that the ox-waggons of the Voortrekkers were outspanned when they gathered in February 1857 for the dedication of the small thatched church which was Pretoria's first building. Here, too, on the following day these early pioneers – symbolized by the brooding bronze statue of a watchful farmer rifle in hand (39) – cheered the first unfurling of the *Vierkleur*, flag of the youthful Zuid-Afrikaansche Republiek. It was this tiny republic which only a few decades later, under the leadership of President Kruger, was to defy the might

of the British Empire. Today the top-hatted statue of 'Oom Paul' (41) dominates Church Square as once he dominated the Afrikaner people in his largely-successful attempts to weld them into a single nation.

An air of such history pervades much of central Pretoria and touches even the most modern buildings. Bronze busts of all the country's white leaders, including former premier J. G. Strydom (43), abound in the centre of the city, forming a progressive link between the past and present. And this link, this sense of history, is at its most tangible in the Voortrekker Monument (44) which caps a hill a few kilometres from the city.

46△ 47▽

◁ 45

In its early years Pretoria was known as the 'City of Roses'; not only did every garden of its often gracious homes boast a rose bed, but ramblers sprawled over hedges and fences. Today it is the 'City of Jacarandas', its wide streets lined with more than 50 000 of these spectacular flowering trees (**45**). Many are the seedling descendants of two jacaranda trees – Pretoria's first – imported from Rio de Janeiro in 1870 for the then princely sum of £10. October and November is jacaranda time when masses of trumpet-shaped flowers transform the leafless branches of each tree into a lilac-blue haze and the falling blossom carpets the ground as if in competition with the sky.

Jacarandas, too, dot the city's 106 gardens and parks, the oldest of which, Burger's Park, was the first piece of land in southern Africa set aside specifically as a park and botanical garden. Opposite it stands Melrose House (**46, 47**), typical of the imposing homes of wealthy Pretorians at the turn of the century. Today it is a historical museum. The stately dwelling, built by the owner of a stage-coach line, has little changed since 1902 when, as the headquarters of Lords Kitchener and Milner, its dining room (**49**) was the venue for the signing of the Treaty of Vereeniging, which ended the second Anglo-Boer War and set South Africa on its first hesitant steps towards union as a

nation. The table (centre) at which the treaty was concluded bears a silver plaque on which are engraved facsimiles of the signatures of all who signed the treaty.

The furnishings of the dining room have remained virtually unchanged since that momentous May day and the ghosts of the doughty republican Boers and their equally intractable imperialistic opponents still seem to crowd the table.

If there are ghosts, one of these will be the shade of Jan Christiaan Smuts, a delegate to the peace negotiations and later one of South Africa's best-known statesmen. Though an international figure in the decades which spanned two World Wars, General Smuts was essen-

48△ 49▽

tially a simple man and it was to the rustic simplicity of Doornkloof (**48**) at Irene, near Pretoria, that he would return to relax and meditate in times of stress. Ironically, in the light of South Africa's position today, Smuts was the guiding mind at the birth of both the League of Nations and the United Nations.

And though the shade of 'Oom Paul' Kruger looms over the 'Jacaranda City', it is Smuts who, more than any other South African, typifies Pretoria's spirit. He was a happy blend of academic and administrator, of soldier and statesman – and having fought to defend the Afrikaner republics then battled with equal dedication to unite Boer and Briton.

51△   52▽

△
50

If South Africa is synonymous with gold, so to investors the world over gold has become synonymous with Kruger Rands (**50**), the one-ounce gold coins which, since 1967, have joined the British sovereign and the French gold franc as the small man's portable form of savings and a hedge against inflation. Marketed at a price slightly higher than that obtaining for gold, the coins are struck (**51**) at the South African Mint, in Pretoria, from blanks from the Germiston refinery.

The blanks are washed and polished (**52**) before being placed in the die where, in the case of 'proof' coins, they are struck twice. The proof Kruger Rands, which sell at a higher premium, are essen-

tially collectors' pieces, snapped up by numismatists and, because a limited number are minted each year, there is usually a waiting list of would-be purchasers. These coins are more carefully sorted and handled (**53**) to ensure they are free of blemish and, literally, in 'mint condition'.

Since the first Kruger Rands were struck, more than 30 million of the gold pieces have been minted. In the record year of 1978, the 6 096 980 coins produced accounted for one quarter of the country's entire gold output. The obverse of each bears a portrait of 'Oom Paul' – from whom the coin takes its name – who ordered the minting of the first gold coins in Pretoria●

53▽

54△ 55▽

In the *domba*, the culmination of the rites which mark the transition of Venda maidens from childhood to maturity, religion and culture create an aesthetically pleasing spectacle (**54**). This is the python dance in which both the serpentine file of participants and the undulation of their arms in accompaniment to the steps, represent the great snake. The tempo of the dance is guided by the bass reverberation of a large wood and hide drum, itself a mystic object (**56, 57**), and two smaller drums, creating a rhythmic tattoo as timeless as the ritual.

The *domba* is the climax to a period of initiation during which the young girls and boys of each Venda village spend several years as part-time inhabitants of a 'play village'. Here they elect their own elders and council and, to a great extent, mirror the pattern of adult routine in preparation for later life.

Tsetse-fly infested the area of the north-eastern Transvaal where the Venda settled, so that they are one of the few black

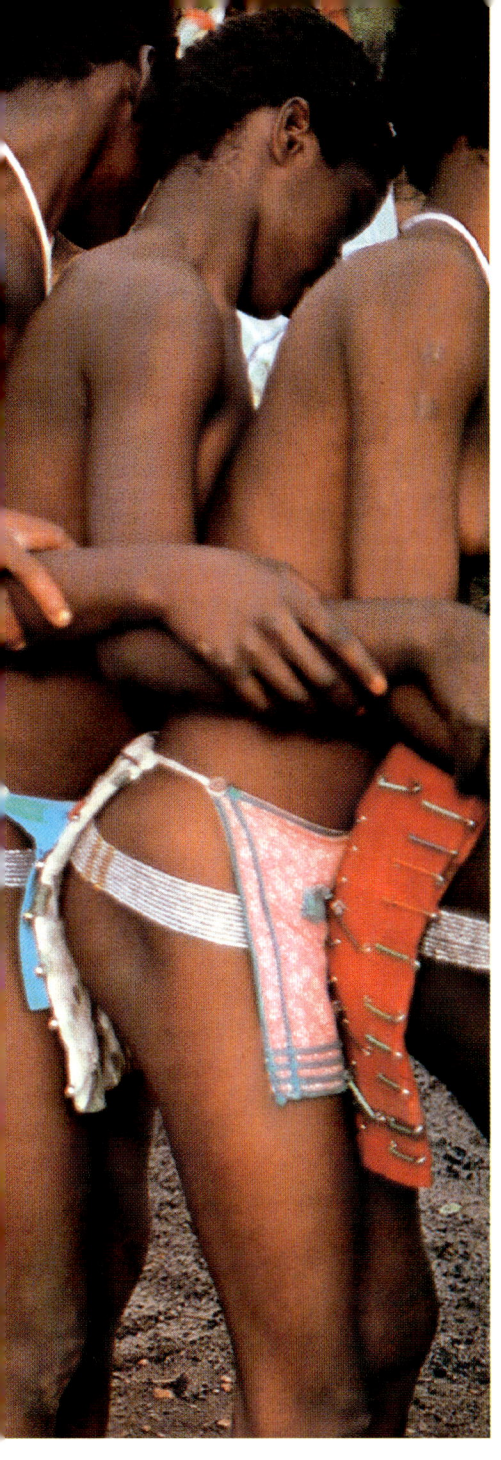

56△ 57▽

58▽ 59▽

tribes to whom the 'riches' of cattle-breeding were denied. Instead they became expert smiths, and their forged iron artefacts became both symbols of wealth and objects of trade. They have retained their tribal identity to a far greater extent than the once-powerful Ndebele, who have been largely absorbed into urban life. The colourful murals of Ndebele homes (**55**) are nevertheless a feature of the southern Transvaal landscape. House-painting – once executed in natural pigments, but today more likely to come from a tin – remains women's work, as does brick-making (**59**), and the spreading of the mud-dung mixture (**58**) which paves living areas.

60△　61▽

The lush softness of subtropical vegetation and stark, multicoloured slashes of sandstone cliff vie for the eye's attention throughout much of the eastern Transvaal. An African Garden of Eden, many parts of the area retain an unspoilt, primeval quality. Nowhere is this more apparent than in the upper reaches of the Blyde River Canyon (**60**) where, over thousands of years, rushing waters have carved a winding path through dolomite and sandstone. In places the canyon is 1,5 km deep, and presents a spectacle which is at once awesome and beautiful.

But in parts of this Lowveld paradise man has battled with Nature, winning rich pasturage (**61**) and ordered forests

63▽

▷
62

from the gentle slopes of the northern fingers of the Drakensberg massif.

When gold was first discovered over 100 years ago in this part of the eastern Transvaal, malaria decimated the inhabitants of several mining camps. Today, the miners have gone, but the echoes of their presence remain in quaint names such as the MacMac Falls (**62**). This 56-metre-high cascade took its name from a nearby mining village, whose inhabitants were so predominantly Scots that, when visiting the area, Transvaal's President Burgers dubbed it 'MacMac'. But though man has imposed his mark, there are still parts (**63**) where the red-gold spears of aloes form a barrier to say: Man go no further.

64△ 65▽

▷
66

Much of this part of the eastern Transvaal was opened up by an international motley of miners, for the pioneer trekkers – the first whites to reach the area in any numbers – moved on, seeking more open, disease-free grazing for their herds. Even the black tribes were daunted by the malarial hazards of the lower-lying parts, so that the land lay unwanted – until the discovery of gold. The first strike, at Eersteling to the west in 1871, sparked a stampede of diggers. And prospectors wise in the experience of the Australian and Californian goldfields, soon probed eastwards tracing the watercourses towards the probable source of the alluvial deposits. In the decade which followed, innumerable deposits of gold were found; some were worked for only a few weeks before their riches were exhausted, others continued to provide a handsome harvest of the precious metal for many years. Around the latter, towns such as Pilgrim's Rest (**64, 66**) soon developed from the tents of the early diggers.

Alluvial gold was found near here in a tributary of the upper

reaches of the Blyde River in 1874, and within weeks a tent town of more than 1 500 prospectors had mushroomed, fed by the relatively easy access of the already-established waggon route from Delagoa Bay to the Lydenburg mines. This was the 'road' made famous by Sir Percy FitzPatrick and today a memorial to his *Jock of the Bushveld* is situated some 5 km outside the town. If the waggon route gave easy access for the diggers and prospectors, it also provided easy pickings for bands of desperadoes who preyed on individual miners and armed waggon trains alike. Some met a swift fate (**65**), others escaped to eventual respectability.

The temptation was great. One nugget weighed 7,8 kg, earning its finder a paltry £750 compared to the R130 000 it would fetch today; and legend has it that in one day enough dust and nuggets were recovered from one of the Bourke's Luck potholes (**67**) to allow its finder to retire wealthy. The last gold was mined at Pilgrim's Rest in 1971.

68 △   **69** ▽

The streams and rivers fed by the waters of the Drakensberg bore wealth other than gold, laying down rich deposits of arable land and still providing irrigation for a wide range of agricultural produce. In recent years tea has become an important crop, and the vast plantations which carpet the countryside in a rich harvest-time green (**68**) between Tzaneen and Barberton, yield enough of the tender tips to brew more than 125 million cups.

And, though the crags and the canyons have remained immune to the plough, many of the slopes and hills of the eastern Transvaal have been given over to intensive forestry. The tangled indigenous woods have been replaced by orderly lines of imported trees – mainly pine and eucalyptus (**69**) – which feed the industrial needs of the nation. But pockets of primal forest remain, the haunt of colourful birds and other fauna which teemed here before their habitat was eroded as man fought to win the land from Nature. Nowhere has the victory been easy and it is only in the last century that the anopheles mosquito and the tsetse-fly have been driven from the lower-lying lands.

When the first trekkers reached the area, the hills and the plains of the eastern Transvaal were alive with game, and early records tell of 'herds of antelope stretching as far as the eye can see'. It was here that the *rinderpest* epidemic first struck,

decimating those self-same herds and almost eliminating South Africa's entire buffalo population. The disease began its savage onslaught in 1896 and in the next two years destroyed more than 2,5 million cattle, as well as hundreds of thousands of antelope and other game. Locally-developed vaccine brought the epidemic under control and finally, in 1903, eliminated it from southern Africa. The crossbreeding of the surviving cattle – such as these being herded kraal-wards near the Lebombo mountains (**70**) – with new, imported strains has led to the Republic's livestock industry comprising more types than are found in any other country. Many of these new breeds are exported.

71△ 72▽ 73▽

The rocky fingers which splay west and north from the eastern mountain spine of South Africa's border with Moçambique provide some of the Transvaal's most spectacular scenery. The outcrops of the Lebombo range are studded with such sites as God's Window and World's View which provide for the traveller the panoramas implicit in their names. Rolling hills and plateaux are rent by sudden gorges (71) whose cliffs are veiled with tenacious trees and undergrowth. Beyond them Africa seems to stretch forever. So splendid and abounding with natural beauty is the area that one popular scenic drive has been dubbed 'the Panorama Road' and from it several spectacular

cascades including the Lisbon Falls (72), can be reached. Typical of the tortuous roads which wind through the area is the Saddleback Pass (73) which climbs from Barberton to Havelock – one of the world's five major sources of asbestos – on the Swaziland border.

Not far from here lie the vast citrus estates of Zebedelia, established soon after World War I and, with more than 650 000 productive trees, arguably one of the world's largest orchards. At harvest time the scent of oranges lies heavy on the still air, a constant reminder that one is never far from subtropical fruits when travelling in the Lowveld. Numerous roadside farmstalls (74) attest further to

75△   76▽

74▽

the wide agricultural riches of the region.

Wild bananas, paw-paws and other tropical fruits already flourished in this vicinity when the Trekkers passed through, for several such exotic fruits had been introduced to this part of Africa centuries earlier by slave traders. That eastern fruits thrive here is underlined by the tremendous success which post-war plantings of litchi trees has met – the orchards near Kaapmuiden produce enough of this delicacy to permit its export.

Known by the people of the area as 'Emanzana' ('healing waters'), Badplaas (75) is a popular recreational resort. Covering nearly 2 000 ha, the spa is cen-

tred on a series of hot sulphur springs, the best-known of several such mineral baths which dot the area. Declared a health resort for the 'everlasting use of the public' in 1893, Badplaas is today a self-contained township. Its hotel, ronda-vels and large camping areas draw thousands of Transvaal holidaymakers, particularly in winter when cooling winds allow the heat and humidity of summer to be temporarily forgotten.

Then, even the lush, subtropical valleys seem briefly temperate; the thorn trees and rank grasses which fringe the hillside roads are sere, the air crisp, if dusty. It is at such times and against such backdrops that the timeless donkey seems

in his element. This unjustly-derided animal – contrary to popular belief, the donkey is neither stupid nor lazy – did much to open up the hinterland of the subcontinent, particularly here in the humidity of the Lowveld.

Its immunity to diseases which debilitated, and often killed, other beasts of burden made the donkey, first introduced to southern Africa in 1656, an ideal form of transport for the early explorers and miners. And though lacking the sheer pulling power of the oxen which comprised most trek-waggon spans, donkeys accompanied most treks – as ubiquitous then as they are on Lowveld roads and dusty trails today (76) ●

77
78△ 79▽

Internationally renowned today as a fine game sanctuary and a major tourist draw-card, the Kruger National Park had an uneasy birth. When the first white men reached the Lowveld it was an animal paradise – the home of vast herds of antelope, elephant, giraffe and the range of predators which accompany the presence of such game. However, the high prices which ivory commanded in Victorian Britain soon led to the decimation of the elephant population; and there was wholesale slaughter of other game too. One hunter claimed to have shot more than 600 springbok in one day – for pleasure and for the pot. By the late 1880s it seemed that game might be obliterated from the Lowveld and, in 1889, though hunting was very much part of the Afrikaner way of life, the Transvaal *Volksraad*, or parliament, banned hunting in certain areas. The move proved largely ineffectual and it took almost a decade before land was set aside between the Crocodile and Sabie rivers as a sanctuary.

But before any suitable administrative structure could be established, the Anglo-Boer War intervened, and it was not until 1902 that practical steps were taken to establish what was then known as the Sabie Game Reserve. Many of the animals which had survived the *rinderpest*

80△

died under the guns of Boer and British soldiers, so that when James Stevenson-Hamilton was appointed as first Chief Game Warden very little game remained.

Nick-named 'Skukuza' – he who scrapes clean – by his black game rangers, Stevenson-Hamilton was to guide the destiny of the 19 019 km² park and its animal inhabitants for the next 44 years. One of the first steps he took was to announce that no shooting would be permitted in the park, and proceeded to put together a team of five white and 50 black rangers – the first of his troops in the unceasing war he was to wage against poachers. Within a year he had successfully prosecuted a group of senior police officers who had hunted game in the park. And though the main offender was fined only £5, 'Skukuza' had shown that he meant business. Today, largely as a result of Stevenson-Hamilton's efforts, the park is the home of a vast cross-section of African wildlife. Giraffe, the world's tallest animals (**77**), sweep sedately through the thorn-scrub in much of the park, sometimes falling prey to lion (**78**) though the king of the veld (**80**) is more likely to dine off one of the many types of antelope such as the massive 300 kg kudu (**79**), whose 1,5 m horns are not always a match for predators. The shy duiker (**81**) is too small for his regal attention and is left to other carnivores.

81▽

82△ 83▽

Though the original boundaries of the Kruger Park were formed in part by rivers where the semi-aquatic hippos gambolled (**82**), animals are no respecters of man's delimitations and until recently the sanctuary's 950 km perimeter has been fenced with cable and barbed wire – as much to keep intruders out as to keep the animals in. But cables and fencing have meant little to the troupes of chacma baboons (**83**) whose scavenging habits around the rest camps have earned them a reputation as pests. Nor has the fencing effectively deterred the elephants (**84, 85**) which have returned to the park and so bred that they must be culled. When the park was established, the activities of poachers had driven these, the largest of all land mammals, away from the Lowveld. Stevenson-Hamilton has recorded the thrill he experienced when he discovered that elephants had returned to the area. He had come upon them early one morning while walking along the river bank and thought, initially, that the two bulky

84△ 85▽

86▽

objects in the water were large rocks, only realizing that they were elephants when they moved – and then remembering that there were no rocks along that particular stretch of river.

Elephants are destructively voracious feeders, consuming as much as 250 kg of grass, shoots and stripped bark each day and thinking nothing of toppling a tree to reach a few tender morsels at the top. Confined as they are within the park, the havoc which they wreak on the vegetation deprives many other animals of sustenance. In recent years their numbers have become so great that their feeding habits have threatened the delicate ecological balance of the browsers and gra-

zers which comprise the bulk of the park's animal population.

The question of grazing in the park is the subject of ongoing research, for not only has the elephant population exploded, but the numbers of predators – lion, leopard, cheetah, hyena and wild dog – also appear to be following an upward trend. This development has been linked to grassland being replaced by bush, thus making prey easier to stalk, and the predator's young easier to feed. The park is also the home of innumerable birds, and some 400 different species have been recorded – including the pied kingfisher (86), seen here limned against a rising moon.

87△ 88▽ 89▽

90▽

The days when the plains of Africa teemed with game are over, and the mass migrations when animals in their hundreds of thousands moved across the Lowveld are no more. But on a daytime safari from one of the rest-camps (**88**) in the Kruger Park one can still thrill to the sight of a herd of zebra, their ordered ranks broken by a lone springbok ram (**87**). There are around 20 rest camps in the park, providing varying degrees of accommodation in terms of comfort. All are fenced to protect the visitor from beasts of prey, and some are noted for the preponderance of particular species of game in the area. Both the Satara and Lower Sabie camps, for instance, are noted for lion, while in the north of the park Letaba and Shingwedzi are regarded as the most likely places to sight elephant. The Marabou stork (**89**), however, is common throughout the park, its large, ungainly body often an indication that the remnants of some predator's kill are present in the bush. Its bald head and neck, combined with its huge powerful bill, make this bird something of a nightmare figure, and the fact that it is often found sharing a feast of carrion with vultures does nothing to enhance it in the minds of most visitors. Yet such scavengers play an important role as the 'dustmen' of the veld, putting the final tidy touches to the remains of a carcass which may have already provided a meal for a lion family, wild dogs and hyenas. Their size, strength and the immense boss of their horns (**90**) which they can wield with devastating accuracy, ensure that buffalo seldom provide a meal for either lion or leopard; the elegantly grace-

91▽

▷
92

93▽

ful waterbuck (**91**, **93**) is more likely to provide leo with his dinner.

In the drier parts of the park, the grotesque baobab (**92**) is found. Its grey trunk with tapering branches is claimed by many black tribes to be the result of God having planted it upside down. Baobabs develop a tremendous girth and one recorded by the missionary David Livingstone measured 25 m around its base.

A deciduous tree, the baobab bears big, scented flowers which are thought to be pollinated by bats. These flowers are followed by large egg-shaped fruits containing a white pulp with a sharp 'cream of tartar' flavour which, when mixed with water, provides a refreshing drink ●

94△ 95▽ 97▽

96▽

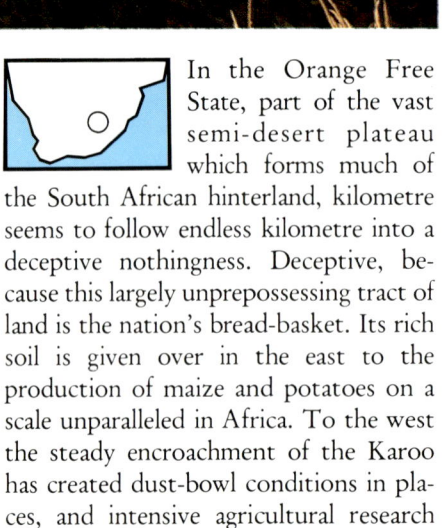

In the Orange Free State, part of the vast semi-desert plateau which forms much of the South African hinterland, kilometre seems to follow endless kilometre into a deceptive nothingness. Deceptive, because this largely unprepossessing tract of land is the nation's bread-basket. Its rich soil is given over in the east to the production of maize and potatoes on a scale unparalleled in Africa. To the west the steady encroachment of the Karoo has created dust-bowl conditions in places, and intensive agricultural research has been devoted to finding a solution to the threat of a desert developing. Vast fields of sunflowers (94) have been planted and these not only help to rehabilitate the soil, but also provide a valuable crop.

The land tends to be flat, broken only occasionally by low hills or koppies, but Nature seems to compensate in the richness of autumn tints with which she adorns the rural landscape. Small catchment dams are frequent, their moist presence often indicated by the ubiquitous willow trees (95) while tall rows of Lombardy poplars stand sentry over the remote fields (97).

If Nature has blessed the Free State landscape with poplars and willows, their warmly glowing colours breaking the monotony, she has saved the richest russets of

▷
98

her palette for an overpoweringly rugged outcrop in the north-eastern part of the province. The Golden Gate (**96, 98**) is, in fact, spectacularly formed of twin peaks set in a massive cliff face. The brilliant range of oranges, yellows and reds which sweep in broad bands across the face and girdle the peaks are the result of thousands of years of interaction between iron oxides present in the rocks. The area surrounding the Golden Gate forms a national park which provides access to the Republic's highest plateau, and the park itself has been re-stocked with many of the animals which were indigenous to the area – the white-tailed gnu, Burchell's zebra and the oribi ●

99△   100▽

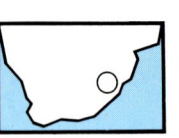

A precipitous wall of rock, its jagged tips frequently hidden by clouds, greeted the first white settlers as they pushed eastward from the Orange Free State with their ox-waggons in search of a route to the fertile lands of the Zulus and the well-watered Tugela basin. This wall was the central and most stubborn section of the Drakensberg, or 'Dragon mountain', and it was to take months of weary trekking before, with their slow, cumbersome waggons, they found a route through the mountains, following what is today the Oliviershoek Pass. It was to take many decades before this section of the moun-

tain massif was tamed, and it is only in recent years that the Sani Pass linking Lesotho and Natal, has been opened.

The Drakensberg is South Africa's largest mountain range, stretching from relatively gentle beginnings in the eastern Cape in a broad 1 064-km sweep to the north and west, finally to peter out in the empty wastes of Namaqualand. But it is with the titanically contorted peaks of the eastern section that the 'Dragon Mountain' is associated. Here the unparalleled

grandeur of soaring rockfaces in the vicinity of Giant's Castle (**99, 101**) is underlined by the wealth of brilliant flora which carpets the lower slopes of the mountains. The rugged wilderness of the scenery is a fitting setting for the Cape vulture (**100**) and other raptors which prey on the inhabitants of the kloofs and krantzes.

Giant's Castle, though not the tallest of the Drakenberg peaks – Injasuti is more than 200 m higher – towers to a massive 3 314 m and is one of the Republic's major mountaineering challenges. The naming of this peak is attributed to Captain Allen Francis Gardiner, a naval officer turned missionary, who probed

101△　102▽

the area in the mid-1830s while trying to establish a mission station at the court of the Zulu king, Dingaan. According to Gardiner, the vast outcrop was a magnificent replica of Edinburgh Castle and the rock of its foundation. Certainly there is a fortress-like quality about this peak which sets it apart. The determined missionary ventured into the mountainous fastness with only a small party, led by a Basuto guide and mounted on a sturdy mountain pony such as may still be seen throughout Lesotho today. This is still the surest method of travel on passes such as the Sani (**102**) and elsewhere in this land of winter snows, which has been dubbed 'the Roof of Africa'.

103△ 104▽ 105△ 106▽

Tumbling streams, fed by melting winter snows and the high annual rainfall which the eastern Drakensberg enjoys, criss-cross the upland plateaux (**105**) to provide a fisherman's paradise of rainbow trout. But this busy rill (**103**) at the head-waters of the Tugela River plays a more significant role than that of providing sport for the visiting angler; and the catch-ment area is more important than catering for the parties of pony-trekkers (**104**). Aptly named Mont-aux-Sources by two intrepid French missionaries in 1836 (they trekked in from the west, across the hostile 'Roof of Africa'), it is the source of South Africa's three great rivers, the Orange, the Vaal and the Tugela, whose waters give life to much of the country's agriculture and industry.

In stark contrast to this part of Natal, much of the Republic's hinterland has a low annual rainfall – indeed one-third of its surface comprises semi-desert. Thus the major rivers are all-important to the economy and dam construction has had

107 ▽

108 ▽

priority for many years. At the turn of the century inland irrigation schemes, fed by the mud and stone dams of the period, provided the means for intensive cultivation, and modern technology with its accompaniment of even bigger dams has permitted the proliferation of this now vital method of agriculture.

Both the Orange and the Tugela rise within a few hundred metres of each other in the typical rock-girt grasslands of the high plateaux (**106**); the Orange draining to the north and west on the start of a winding course which will take it 2 300 km to the Atlantic, a course during which it is joined by the mighty Vaal. The Tugela's route is shorter, though it covers 560 km before reaching the Indian Ocean – a mere 220 km from its source. A substantial part of its volume is lost to the sea, in spite of a series of massive dams and other measures introduced to conserve its flow of 6 800 million litres a day. This is more than five times the volume of the Vaal and, in flood, gives the river a strength which even in recent years has washed away road and rail bridges.

It is water showing its more subtle force that has honeycombed sections of the limestone strata, deep beneath the peaks, to provide a pot-holer's wonderland (**107**) of underground streams and caverns. Here over hundreds of thousands of years, snow and rain have found their way into cracks and fissures, enlarging them into a smooth-walled labyrinth many parts of which remain unplumbed by man. That the upper portions of these caves and subterranean passages gave shelter to the ancestors of the modern speleologist is attested by many rich archaeological finds of Stone Age artefacts. More recently, within written memory, some provided homes for clans of Bushmen, whose only memorials are the rock paintings which they executed in rich pigments – colours often still so fresh today as to vie with those of a mountain cloudscape (**108**) touched by the dying sun ●

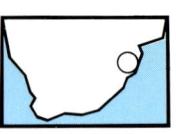

Considered to be the largest estuarine system in Africa, St Lucia is a 35 000-ha saline coastal lagoon fed by the rivers which drain northern Natal and by water which seeps from the sea via the adjacent sand catchments (**109**). Although very shallow, with an average depth of less than one metre, droughts take place every several years, causing considerable fluctuation in the water level: rivers stop flowing and water is lost through evaporation, lowering the level to below that of the sea. Sea water flows into the lagoon and under extreme conditions, the salt from it becomes so concentrated that in places the water can become three times as salty as the sea. Conversely, during wet cycles the lake level rises to above that of the sea and water flows out of St Lucia. As a result, most of the lake water can be fresh.

The duration of the full wet-dry cycle is about a decade, and the constant changes in salinity and lake level have resulted in a very dynamic ecosystem. In the past, it was feared that St Lucia was deteriorating because of poor land-use practices in the catchment areas, aggravated by droughts. Now, extensive scientific research and an understanding of the system have proved these fears to be unfounded. Every plant and animal occurring in St Lucia has a preferred range of salinity within which it thrives and beyond which it dies: at low salinities submerged water plants thrive and form a food-rich habitat

111△ 112▽

113▽

which attracts many ducks; at higher salinities, the lake teems with estuarine fish and fish-eating birds. Some 6 000 white pelicans (112) breed in the northern wilderness of the lake, while fish eagles, herons, gulls and terns are abundant. During periods of high salinity the plankton-rich waters attract as many as 60 000 flamingoes (111), whose pink masses create a spectacular sight.

A popular misconception is that St Lucia, because it is so shallow, is silting up. In reality, very little sediment enters the lake: the sediment-rich waters of the Mkuze River are filtered by the papyrus and reed beds in the Mkuze swamp north of the lake.

St Lucia remains one of South Africa's premier angling venues. In addition, some of its 800 hippos (110), 1 500 crocodiles (113) and several of its fish eagles can be observed from the 'Narrows'. A scenically beautiful drive along the Eastern Shores – the barrier

between sea and lake – to Cape Vidal reveals 180-m-high coastal dunes clad in luxurious dune forest, and grassy plains interspersed with wetlands harbouring reedbuck, kudu, waterbuck, buffalo and the elusive black rhino.

At Cape Vidal the sheltering reef protects a colourful diversity of fish, seaweed and other marine life. North of here are the long stretches of golden beach for which this region is well known.

One of the three oldest reserves in Africa, St Lucia's variety of scenery, habitat, plant and animal life has earned it recognition under the Ramsar Convention as a 'wetland of international importance'.

114△   115▽   117▷

116▽

Though almost as many species of birds have been recorded at Lake St Lucia and its environs as in the entire British Isles and western Europe, these represent only slightly more than half of South Africa's avian population. Some 850 different species – or one tenth of all the world's known birds – have been observed in South Africa. The bulk of these breed here and many are indigenous. But statistics cannot begin to convey the magic of a carpet of lesser flamingoes, their deep pink plumage glowing like a sunset as they wade across a stretch of mud-flat; nor can they begin to tell of the feathered glory of many woodland species such as this weaver (118) which, when disturbed, take to the air in a flurry of yellows and blacks. Even the apparent ungainliness of this immature pink-backed pelican (114), more prolific in the St Lucia area than elsewhere in southern Africa, has its own special enchantment. Pelicans, though cumbersome in moments of take-off – their large webbed feet paddle frantically – have a winged grace of their own once airborne. In contrast, the jackal buzzard (115) is a masterful flyer, making graceful use of its powerful wings and broad tail to soar elegantly through the air.

The pelican's long, heavy bill – immortalized by the humorous poet Ogden Nash – surmounts a soft naked

118▽

pouch which serves the dual purpose of 'netting' the fish and aquatic animals on which it preys, and holding these (117) until it is ready to eat them. Pelicans have refined cooperative effort to an art when fishing, and dozens of the birds will form a semi-circular line, beating the water with their wings and feet to drive their quarry in front of them, where they can scoop up their prey in the lower half of their capacious bills.

Physical adaptation, mirrored in the pelican's eating habits, manifests itself in a different way in the case of birds of prey. The Cape vulture (116) has a powerful, sharp beak, evolved to allow it successfully to feed on the entrails of carcasses. Like pelicans, vultures will feed in packs, often fighting viciously over a meal. Vultures are, however, extremely fastidious and bathe daily, often flying considerable distances to find water in which to wash – a problem the pelican does not have to face.

119△ 120▽ 121▽

Each mid-winter, in a mysterious migration whose pattern has remained unchanged in the span of written history, vast and concentrated shoals of two-year-old pilchards pass through the coastal waters of southern Natal. Often this mass of fish is swept so close inshore and in such a density that beach-front housewives – and seemingly half the coastal population – rush into the shallows with baskets and basins to reap the silver harvest of the 'sardine run'. So intense an excitement does the event evoke that otherwise-staid business executives have been known to discard their shoes and socks, roll neatly-pressed trousers above their knees and join the spray-filled fun. Others, more serious in their approach to the random harvest, use trek nets (**119, 122**) in which they haul literally tonnes of the young fish from the surf with each trawl.

The Sardine run, which is followed by a train of swooping sea-birds as well as sharks and other large fish, disappears north of Durban and it is thought that the survivors of the winged, finned and two-legged predators are carried southwards to the Cape by the warm Agulhas Current. Its waters, rich in a wide range of marine life, provide endless hours of pleasure for scuba-divers and rod-anglers (**120, 121**) whose catches range from the mighty marlin and swordfish to the smaller species often sold in 'bunches' (**123**).

This broad spectrum of marine life provides tremendous potential for scientific exploration, and the Oceanographic Research Institute – the only such body in South Africa, which is privately-funded – probes Natal's waters to harvest knowledge from the sea.

If the coastal and off-shore waters add to man's knowledge, the rich alluvial coastal plains of Natal add to his or her girth. For these are the sugar lands (**125**) whose cane, first planted here in 1851, has made South Africa one of the world's 'big five' producers of what was once known as 'white gold'. The warm humid climate and fertile earth of the hills and valleys of the north coast are ideal for this towering

122△　123▽

124△　125▽

relative of the field grasses and, under Natal conditions, it gives one of the highest yields of sap anywhere in the world. So intensive is the cultivation that even the steepest slopes are planted and here, where a fourwheeled-drive tractor cannot hold its course, the planters revert to an earlier method of ploughing – with oxen (**124**).

The cane fields are also among the world's last outposts of another earlier form of traction – the narrow-gauge steam locomotive. These elderly engines – several of them relics of the *eisenbahnen* of Germany's African colonies – carry the cut cane to the stamping mills where it is crushed and the sugar-rich sap extracted.

126△ 127▽ 128▽ 129▷

Natal is South Africa's smallest province, covering only 8% of the entire area of the Republic, but it boasts the greatest number of game reserves, devoting nearly 250 000 ha to the conservation of its indigenous flora and fauna. It was from the thorny scrubland of its Hluhluwe Reserve that the re-population of Africa with the white rhinoceros (126) began. This relatively placid giant – it is the smaller black rhino which has a deserved reputation for bad-tempered aggressiveness – was once widespread throughout the savannahs of southern and central Africa, its range extending as far as southern Ethiopia.

Rhinoceros horn – not actually a horn at all, but densely-compacted, fibrous hairs – commanded princely prices in the Far East, where it was in great demand as an aphrodisiac. As a result, the white rhino was hunted almost to extinction. Its gentler mien – and the more open scrub in which it dwelt – made this stumpy-legged mammal a far easier target than its black relative. By 1930, only 28 were known to exist; and these were to be found only in the northern basin of the Hluhluwe Reserve, saved from extinction by the strictly-enforced preservation laws which had operated there since 1897. Slowly Hluhluwe's pitifully small herds were built up and from this stock white rhinos were re-introduced to other parks

130▽

– first in South Africa and later in other countries. In recent years they have even transcended political boundaries as welcomed immigrants to parts of black Africa where the Republic's other 'white' species is anathema.

Though Hluhluwe proved a haven for the white rhino, Natal's preservation laws were introduced too late to save the elephant and in this part of South Africa the last tusker trumpeted his defiance of man in the 1800s. However, in mid-1981 moves were initiated to re-introduce elephants to Hluhluwe from the Kruger National Park.

The wide range of physical and climatic conditions which the tiny province enjoys has not only contributed to the preservation of other rare species such as the oribi, but has allowed most forms of wildlife indigenous to the sub-continent to flourish in one or other of the 27

reserves. Thus a wide range of aquatic birds inhabit Natal lagoons and lakes, such as that at Ndumu (**127**), while impala (**128**) – renowned for their spectacular leaps when alarmed – are to be found in most reserves. So, too, is the brown hyena (**130**), a nocturnal scavenger whose powerful jaws can crush even the largest bones to powder. And though not numerous – they are a comparatively rare species even within the sanctuaries of all Africa's game parks – cheetah (**129**) inhabit most of the savannah reserves. Their skins are still prized as part of a Zulu warrior's regalia, though no longer a symbol that the wearer has slain a specimen of this, the world's fastest predator.

131△ 132▽

133△ 134▽

Where in the first half of this century Natal was to ensure the continued existence of the white rhino, the first decades of the 19th century saw the land spawn death. For this was the anvil on which was forged the Zulu nation and its military machine, an army responsible for human slaughter unprecedented in southern Africa. Entire tribes were annihilated by its onslaught – and it even withstood the might of Britain.

Today the Zulu nation – some 200 clans – is South Africa's largest ethnic grouping, comprising a fifth of the country's citizens. Only a relatively small number of its people live and work in KwaZulu, the fragmented

135 ▽ 136 ▷

'homeland' constituted in the 1970s as part of the white Nationalists' 'Grand Apartheid' design and which, in 1994, was reincorporated into the province of KwaZulu, Natal. The wider and more historic national home is known as Zululand, the region that lies to the north of the Tugela River – a country of lovely hills and valleys fringed in the east by flattish, humid coastal terraces and by the limpid waters of the Indian Ocean. The land's agricultural potential is high and it enjoys a high rainfall, but it lacks industry or mineral wealth which could support the burgeoning population, and many of the people of Zululand – particularly the men – have to seek employment in the industrial PWV region. Thus for much of each year its rural areas are largely the preserve of women and children (**131**). In spite of considerable cultural 'westernization', in many respects the Zulus remain staunch traditionalists and, as a result, agricultural output is not drastically affected by the absence of the men. For, by custom, the fields are cultivated by the women, and livestock are tended by the youths. To the women, too, fall the tasks of basket-work, brewing and moulding the often massive earthenware pots (**132** and **133**) used for storage of foodstuffs and to contain the highly nutritious beer, which is both socially and ritually important.

When the tasks of daily living or the pastoral activities of the herder are completed, both womenfolk and youths (**135**) find time for beautification. The elaborate traditional head-dresses of the Zulu matron are the result of long and painstaking effort. Created from ochre and fibre, these splendid coiffures are often built up around a wooden framework, or may be structured from a twisted 'rope' of cloth (**136**) to reveal its eventual inverted cone (**134**), given added glory by bands of elaborate bead-work, which may have a meaning or be purely ornamental.

137△ 138▽ 139△ 140▽

More than any other of southern Africa's black peoples it is the Zulus who have captured the world's imagination. Not only has the prowess of their warriors become legendary, but their noble bearing, enhanced by the richness of their tribal costume, has made them popular subjects for the illustrator from the earliest days of white exploration. Originally a vassal clan of the powerful Mthethwas, their rise to power began with Shaka, who assumed the leadership of the Zulus in 1816. Using this as a power base, he steadily gained control of the neighbouring 300 loosely knit tribes and clans, forging them into a kingdom whose line of direct succession stretches unbroken to the present monarch.

Shaka, despot though he was to become, was both a brilliant administrator and military tactician. Developing the administrative system he had inherited from his predecessor, Shaka split the young men of the various clans into regiments according to age, instead of the previous family allegiances. In doing so he ensured their loyalty to the throne rather than to the headmen. These regiments literally grew up together, living in their own kraals with their own herds, and were forbidden to marry until they were 40 years old. Even then, the marriages were largely controlled by the King, who ensured that such alliances were with suitable women's 'regiments'. While no believer in sexual equality, Shaka regulated the lives of the Zulu women as closely as he did the men.

But such organized regiments, as many another militarist has found, require more than discipline and drill. Today's tribal dances (**139**) were part of the warrior's parade-ground routine. It served to keep them occupied when not being let loose on the surrounding tribes. In his army, each regiment or *Impi* was distinguished by its uniform and pattern of cow-hide shield. The short stabbing *assegai*, introduced to replace the spears which had previously been hurled from ineffectual distances, wreaked havoc in the hands of his warriors. Tribe after tribe was

141▽   **142**▷

conquered. Their chiefs were killed and the captives drafted into his army, while the women and children joined the losers' cattle as part of the spoils of war. In so developing his kingdom, Shaka annihilated entire tribes and forced others to flee before military might in what became known as the *Difaqane*, or forced migrations.

Shaka was murdered in 1828, but in 12 short years he had forged the Zulu empire and created the legend that lingers today. And though his people have become westernized in terms of dress – so that even a royal hunt in which the tribesmen act as beaters (**141**) lacks the panoply of its past – there are events, such as tribal dances and displays (**137**, **138** and **140**), when the magic of the legend is recaptured. And some customs, too, remain; single women still go bare-breasted (**142**) and only married women wear the elaborate ochre head-dress (**143**) which, like the rural beehive huts, is so much part of the traditional Zulu image ●

143▽

144△ 145▽

At the start of every school holiday, or whenever there is a long weekend (in the South African context, this is when a public holiday occurs, just before or after a weekend – preferably one at either end), the inhabitants of the northern regions embark on a mass exodus to the coastal city of Durban. Its main attraction, the 'Golden Mile' (144 and 145), is a glittering 6-km-long stretch of seafront crammed with just about every diversion the hedonist could wish for. Here are amusement parks, pavilions, piers and pools, round-the-clock nightspots and fine eating places, emporiums and colourful markets, fountains, emerald lawns and graceful walkways. And, of course, acres of golden beach.

And for inland dwellers of the winter-dry Free State and Transvaal Highveld, the lure of the sea is understandable. The often cloying humidity is momentarily forgotten as one gapes in wonderment at the antics of the bottlenose dolphins at Sea World (home to the Oceanographic Research Institute) (146), or as one gasps in awe at the toothy menace of a Zambezi shark (147) in one of the giant tanks of the oceanarium. Many of the sharks on show have been rescued from special

146△

147△   148▽

nets set offshore along parts of the Natal coastline to protect bathers and as part of an ongoing research programme, while income from the complex also helps to fund marine research.

But in spite of its pleasure-palace façade (148), Durban is a major industrial and commercial centre, and one of the southern hemisphere's busiest trade outlets. It was as a harbour that South Africa's third largest city had its beginnings: as Port Natal, it saw the arrival in 1824 of Natal's first white settlers. Today nearly 40 million tons of cargo – sugar, fruit, coal and anthracite, manganese, manufactured goods – are processed by the dockyards.

149△ 150▽   151△

Though Durban is the hedonist of South Africa's cities, it is also the most 'British'. Its centre is dominated by an unmistakably late-Victorian city hall which, with its attendant palm trees and flower-sellers (149), has all the majesty of the 'Raj' – though not completed until 1910. And to many, as they take 'tiffin' on the cooler heights of Berea in subtropical gardens filled with the chatter of mynahs, it is still a last outpost of the Empire.

For nearly two decades after the arrival of the first white settlers in 1824, Britain wanted neither Durban nor Natal – this despite its naming in 1835 after the then Governor of the Cape. It was not until 1842, when the settlement had been absorbed as part of the early Boer Republic of Natalia, that Britain decided to annex the port and its surrounds. Even then they only did so to deny the Boers an easy entry for arms and ammunition which the authorities at the Cape feared might be used against them, either by the hostile

152▽

frontier tribes – with whom they were in constant conflict – or by the Boers themselves.

Today, yachts on the placid beach (**150**) and the modern metropolis with its veins of roads and rail tracks (**151**) reflect no legacy of those troubled times. But in 1842, it was here – where only four years earlier the Trekkers had helped the small English settlement beat off Dingaan's *impis* – that the annexing forces were besieged by the Boers. In an epic ride, a young waggon-driver and lieutenant in the Port Natal Volunteers summoned help from Grahamstown. In ten days Dick King rode some 960 km to raise reinforcements from the frontier garrison and, returning by sea with the colonial troops, was acclaimed as the 'Saviour of Natal'. The troops then raised the siege – and went on to impose British rule in at least part of Natal. Disappointingly, perhaps, the war-like costumes of the city's ricksha boys (**152**) bear scant resemblance to the kilts of their fighting forebears – owing more to tourism than to tradition.

153△ 154▽ 155▽

The high-rise sophistication of Durban's seafront (**153**) is five centuries and a world away from the desolate swamp observed from afar by Vasco da Gama. And the modern craft in Durban's ground harbour bear only a remote resemblance to the trio of timber craft, headed by the *São Gabriel*, in which his expedition traversed these waters at Christmas 1497, to name the land they discovered *Terra do Natal*. There is no record that he landed here while establishing the sea-route to India. But long before the settlement at Port Natal, other seafarers anchored in the waters sheltered by the Bluff, the first links in the chain of Durban's continuing maritime importance.

Despite the preponderance of pleasure-seekers who gambol among the ocean rollers (**153**) or take to the gentler waters of the Golden Mile's seafront (**156**). Durban is essentially a port city. Until the establishment in the 1970s of the massive minerals terminal at Richards Bay, 187 km northwards, Durban handled more annual tonnage than the combined total of all the Republic's other ports; the naval base at Salisbury Island – briefly abandoned after World War II, but resuscitated in recent years – was one of the largest in the southern hemisphere; and its waterfront dives and nightclubs were notorious across the Seven Seas. Today the latter are the haunt of semi-

156 ▽

157 ▽

158 ▽

sedate visitors rather than sea-dogs. Glittering disco-dancers have replaced their less reputable sisters of the earlier days. And Durban's seafront is graced by some of the world's most elegant hotels, many staffed by Natal Indians in resplendent garb (**154**).

But the same sea which gives its beneficence to the yachtsmen and bathers has its ugly side, and the waters off the Natal coast have claimed innumerable ships. It was from Durban in July 1909 that the *Waratah* sailed to her fate, giving rise to one of the sea's major, and still unsolved mysteries. The twin-screw steamship, with a crew of 119 and luxurious accommodation for 100 pas-

sengers, was one of the largest and most modern on the run from London to Australia. On her second return voyage from Durban on July 26, she passed and exchanged flag signals with the *Clan McIntyre* on the following day; and she has never been seen since. No wreckage or other sign of her has ever been dis-

covered and it is believed that the *Waratah* foundered in some freak storm, beaten into the maw of the deep by one of the giant waves for which these waters are notorious. Fortunately the distant forces which spawn such waves allow of their mellowing before they reach the shores, and many stretches on this part of the Natal coast offer fine surfing (**158**).

Thus it is as a pleasure ground that its modern visitors remember Durban's seafront pool and playground (**157**) and its serried ranks of graceful yachts, its funland, its splendid sporting facilities, its luxury hotels and fine restaurants, many of which pay delectable tribute to the city's Indian heritage.

◁159   160△   161▽

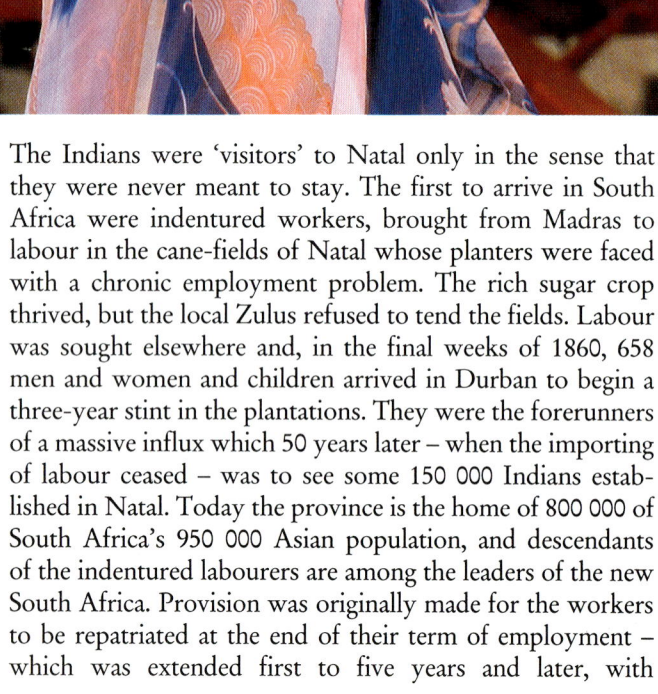

The Indians were 'visitors' to Natal only in the sense that they were never meant to stay. The first to arrive in South Africa were indentured workers, brought from Madras to labour in the cane-fields of Natal whose planters were faced with a chronic employment problem. The rich sugar crop thrived, but the local Zulus refused to tend the fields. Labour was sought elsewhere and, in the final weeks of 1860, 658 men and women and children arrived in Durban to begin a three-year stint in the plantations. They were the forerunners of a massive influx which 50 years later – when the importing of labour ceased – was to see some 150 000 Indians established in Natal. Today the province is the home of 800 000 of South Africa's 950 000 Asian population, and descendants of the indentured labourers are among the leaders of the new South Africa. Provision was originally made for the workers to be repatriated at the end of their term of employment – which was extended first to five years and later, with

freedom to choose their employer, to ten – but few of them wished to return to the poverty of their birthplace.

Most of these Indians were Tamil-speaking Hindus and Muslims, and they still comprise the bulk of the Republic's Asian population. However, their growing community also attracted a substantial number of Gujarati traders who soon established thriving businesses throughout Natal, causing concern among their white counterparts who saw them as a competitive threat. It was to protect these Gujarati interests that a young Indian lawyer, Mohandas K. Gandhi, arrived in South Africa. And it was here, later, that as Mahatma and leader of the Indian political struggle, he developed his philosophy of passive resistance, or *Satyagraha*. That he overcame both prejudice and political power-play, in which the Indian was controversial pawn, is part of South Africa's history. And the Indians' presence as part of the land's business and professional community is a measure of the first success of a philosophy

162 ▽   163 ▷

164 ▽

which was eventually to win for India her independence and which was to spread around the world.

Many of South Africa's Indians maintain close links with relatives in their land of origin; but even to those who do not, it still looms large as the source of both their culture and their way of life. Women still wear the graceful sari as they buy or sell the wares of the market (**159**), its airs redolent with the smell of curry and the scent of spices. At Durban's Grey Street mosque (**160**), the largest in the southern hemisphere, the men and women still worship strictly segregated according to sex (**161**, **162**). The splendour of oriental pageantry, alive in colour and equipage, still radiates from the many Hindu festivals and ceremonies (**163**) which are celebrated throughout Natal. And even the brilliance of a flower-seller's blooms (**164**) seems to echo the tropical richness of the land from which the first poor labour-force arrived giving not only their expected sweat, but adding to the mélange of South Africa's cultures.

Its rolling landscapes often a seemingly-endless patchwork of tilled fields and pasturage (**165**), there is little in Transkei today to remind the traveller that here, less than 150 years ago, a 17-year-old girl led a powerful nation to the brink of mass suicide. Her name was Nonquase and she grew up in a rondavel with its surround of aloes, very similar to those that dot the countryside today (**166**).

But Nonquase had a vision. She claimed that a great wind would spring up and bring forth ancestral warriors to drive the white man into the sea. To the Xhosa tribes, who had been engaged in a pro-

167△　168▽

tracted series of wars with the colonists for more than 50 years, this was heady stuff. Even Nonquase's pronouncement that before the spectral wind of change would blow they must kill all their cattle and destroy their grain, did not deter the tribesfolk. Herds were decimated, food was destroyed and, when the fateful day in 1858 arrived – nothing happened. In the famine which followed, tens of thousands died, and Xhosa might was broken.

The land has recovered and the sea still offers a fulsome harvest on Transkei's Wild Coast (**167, 168**). But the spirit of Nonquase may well have smiled wryly when, in 1976, Pretoria granted Transkei its 'independence'.

169△ 170△ 171▽

To the rural people of the Transkei, the political manipulations of the past few decades have brought few changes, either in the pattern or the standard of their living. In spite of sustained efforts by the social engineers to encourage industrial development, jobs remain so scarce that a substantial number of Xhosas have to find work on the mines or in the cities of the north. Nor has the exchange of black for white rule necessarily improved amenities, particularly in the remoter areas where, without electricity, women must still collect wood for fuel (**169**). As in other black tribes, wood-gathering is only one of many tasks which is

the woman's traditional lot; she must cultivate the fields and make many of her domestic implements such as these simple brooms (**173**), besides carrying out the domestic chores expected of her western counterpart. The compact family structure means that the older married women will cook and brew beer, leaving to the

younger women in the family the more energetic tasks. But even here, in a land where poverty remains the norm, older women must help till the land, saving the habitual pipe of tobacco (**172**) for reflective moments. Pipe-smoking comes with seniority, while married status is proclaimed by a swathe of turban still often seen. The often sparse harvests reaped by the women are becoming even poorer as a result of erosion (**171**). Contour-ploughing (**175**) is assisting with recovery of the land, but the problem still exists. Prior to the Transkei's independence several agricultural education schemes were introduced; but, mainly because cultivation is traditionally women's work, these re-

◁172 173△ 174▽

175▽

ceived remarkably little support from the tribesmen so that progress has been slow.

For the boys and youths of the Transkei, however, tending the cattle and other livestock is the main activity. Among the rural tribesfolk particularly, cattle remain the measure of a man's wealth and still are central to the ritual of *lobola*, the 'bride price' which a prospective husband pays to his father-in-law's family to compensate them for the loss of a daughter. Many customs are gradually disappearing under the onslaught of white culture and values borrowed from it, but the system of *lobola* in one form or another is retained by most rural blacks – as are the initiation ceremonies which

mark the transition from adolescence to adulthood.

Among some tribes the ritual of circumcision has disappeared entirely and a spell working on the mines has effectively replaced it. But among the rural Xhosa an age-old formula of initiation is still followed in which the

young men, known as *abakwetha*, their heads shaved and their bodies painted with river clay (**170, 174**), live apart from the community in special thatched lodges. While the wounds of their circumcision heal, they are taught the mores and behaviour expected of them as adult members of society, and are taught tribal history as well.

At the end of their period of initiation, the thatched lodge – one of the few beehive structures which the Xhosa have retained from their earlier period – is ceremoniously burned and the *abakwetha* race each other to a river, to cleanse themselves of the clay. They have reached maturity.

176△ 179▷

177△ 178▽

To the young Xhosa in the years before Nonquase's prophecy broke the might of his tribe, the attainment of manhood meant becoming a warrior. His days of leisurely herding – their monotony perhaps broken by watching a sunset bird at the river mouth (**176**) or catching shellfish on the Pondoland coast (**179**) – were over.

Among the first black tribes who the white explorers encountered as they drove eastward from their tiny enclave in the Cape, a warrior concept was already well-entrenched. With good cattle country in increasingly short-supply, the Xhosa-speaking peoples were already engaged in inter-clan squabbling. Their subsequent conflicts with the white settlers shared something of the same imperatives – land and water for man and stock. The air of calm tranquillity of the Amatola mountain range and the pastorally idyllic scenes which mark the land between the Great Fish and the Kei rivers (**177**) belie the often bloody conflict here which marked the late 18th Century and

much of the 19th. The Great Fish River was once the eastern frontier of the Cape and the scene of many clashes between black and white. Today this division still pertains, for the river forms the western boundary of the Ciskei, which until recently also existed as a separate 'state'.

Like the Transkei, the Ciskei is also inhabited by the Xhosa. It came into being as the result of a bloody family quarrel more than two centuries ago. In the mid-18th century, Galeka, heir to the Xhosa chieftainship, launched a rebellion against his father Phalo. Loyalties were divided, but Phalo, aided by his favourite son Rarabe, put down the uprising after a series of skirmishes in which both sides sustained heavy losses. Though Phalo and Rarabe were victorious, they migrated with their supporters across the Kei to create a geographic split in the tribe which continues to this day.

The area in which the victors settled was the battle-ground on which a series of nine protracted clashes – known to history as the Frontier Wars and spanning more than a century – were fought. It was here that white and black, both hungry for land, first came into extended contact. And it was here, too, in the shadow of the Amatola Mountains, that one of the most bitter of the wars broke out, and ostensibly for the pettiest of reasons. It began in 1846 with the ambush of a patrol sent to arrest a tribesman who had allegedly stolen an axe. The Xhosa chose this incident as an excuse to invade the Colony and made off with many head of cattle. In retalliation a punitive expedition of colonial forces, aided by tribes hostile to the Xhosa, set out but was hampered by drought. The Xhosa withdrew to the mountains, remaining undefeated until a burgher force invaded what is today the Transkei and claimed for the Colony all land west of the Kei River. The War of the Axe – though not the last of the Frontier Wars – was part of the gradual process which led to peaceful co-existence (**178**) between black and white in this part of the Cape ●

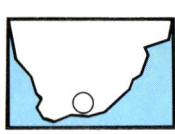

The pin-cushion of spires and steeples of more than 40 churches and chapels which prick its skyline, has earned Grahamstown the nickname 'City of the Saints'. But 'City of the Sinners' might be no less appropriate, for half of the first stone structure built in this former garrison town was a gaol. In the unsettled days of the Frontier Wars, Col. John Graham, who established the town as his headquarters in 1812, probably needed the cells as much for his 'rough soldiery' as he did for the Xhosas of the Zuurveld where he had come to impose an uneasy peace.

His task of policing the vast tract of land between Algoa Bay and the inland mountain ranges, and containing the cattle-hungry Xhosa tribes behind an arbitrary eastern boundary, proved almost impossible. Time and again the blacks probed westward and threatened the Cape Colony. In these circumstances, and to provide a protective buffer, the British government devised a major immigration scheme. This came to frui-

tion eight years after Colonel Graham had established his garrison.

The arrival of the 1820 Settlers at Algoa Bay on April 20 is commemorated in one of several stained-glass windows (**182**) in the Methodist Church. St George's Cathedral (**180**), incorporates part of the original church – used as an ammunition depot and a refuge for women and children when Grahamstown was threatened in the 6th Frontier War of 1834-35. St John's Anglican Church in Bathurst (**183**) – the oldest Anglican church in South Africa to remain unaltered – served a similar use before it was even completed. The arrival of the Settlers had spurred the Xhosa to more

◁180   182△   183△   184▽

frequent raids rather than deterring them, and for many years the brass bell of St John's (**181**) was as likely to call the local inhabitants to arms as to call parishioners to church.

Life was not easy for these early immigrants who left their indelible stamp not only on that part of the eastern Cape still known as 'Settler Country', but on South Africa as a whole. Though they were given free passage from Britain, were issued with seeds and implements at low cost, and were to be given title deeds to the lands they occupied, everything seemed to conspire against their success.

Severe drought, crop failure, floods in 1823 and constant attacks by the Xhosa throughout the first five years, almost caused the collapse of the new settlement. However, the establishment of several forts and of villages such as Bathurst, then the administrative centre of the Zuurveld, was still made possible. A steady improvement in conditions from 1825 onwards marked the beginning of a prosperous era for the community.

Outside the 'locations', as the lands they occupied were called, farms were bought and the hiring of black labour allowed expansion into pastoral farming. The wool industry flourished and skilled artisans practised their trades in the towns. Churches were built all over the district, and schools and academies were started in towns such as Salem and Grahamstown. Though the 6th Frontier War of 1834 cost many lives and devastated the Albany District, as the Zuurveld had come to be known, the survivors rebuilt their community. By 1864 the area had become so stable, and so important, that the Cape Parliament felt safe enough to hold a session in Grahamstown – the only time it did not sit in Cape Town.

Today the hill-top site, a few kilometres outside Bathurst, from which Col. Jacob Cuyler allotted 'locations' to the first immigrants, is capped by a topograph showing their sites in relation to the outspread (**184**) 'Settler Country' ●

185△   186▽

When the Portuguese cartographer Manuel Perestrelo, charged with charting the south and east coast of Africa, reached Plettenberg Bay in 1597, he named it Bahia Formosa, or 'beautiful bay'. It was not the first name bestowed on this curving stretch of shore, nor was it the last, but it was certainly the most appropriate. For Plettenberg Bay (185) - so dubbed by Governor Joachim van Plettenberg in 1778 thereby ending its multi-named confusion - is regarded by many as the jewel of the Garden Route.

This verdant expanse of lakes, rivers and forests stretches from Swellendam in

187△ **188**▽

the west to Humansdorp in the east and is framed by the warm Indian Ocean and the rugged Outeniqua and Tsitsikama mountains. And where Durban is the mecca of the frenetic pleasure-seeker, the estuaries and beaches of the Garden Route provide a tranquil retreat for the angler. He may cross the Storms River Mouth suspension bridge (**186**) to the privacy of sea-girt rocks shared only with the seals – or seek a silent cove of sand.

Survivors of the shipwrecked *São Gonçalo* who spent almost a year on the shores of Plettenberg Bay before being rescued in 1630 saw the area as a lotus-land. Animals and wild fruits abounded in the primeval forests, there were fish

aplenty in the rivers and lagoons, and the climate was balmy. On a large slab of sandstone they carved the name Perestrelo had chosen, and though it has passed from usage, the stone remains with its words 'Bahia Formosa'.

Many parts of the lush Tsitsikama Forest – which with the Knysna Forest covers 36 400 ha to form South Africa's largest woodland – have remained almost unchanged since then. In places it marches to the very edge of the shallow coastal cliffs (**187**). But the vast stands of yellowwood, stinkwood, ironwood and indigenous trees proved a magnet for the timber-hungry settlements of the Cape.

Ten years after Van Plettenberg had given the bay its permanent name, the sound of the axe replaced the call of the Knysna loerie to echo among the trees, and stacked baulks of timber lined the sands over which the luxury Beacon Island Hotel (**188**) today stands guard.

189△ 190▽

The timber wharves have long since gone from Plettenberg Bay and the wood and canvas of holiday-makers' deck chairs have replaced the spars and sails of the coasters. At Knysna – the other main source of beams and boards for the 19th-century building boom – timber and tourism go hand in hand. The placidity of its lagoon – a pleasure haven for small craft and light-tackle anglers – is in sharp contrast to the angry currents and waves which pound the narrow entrance of The Heads (**189**). The sleepy-hollow weekday atmosphere of the town's main street gives no indication – save for the distant whine of a circular saw – that Knysna is also the home of several factories, where some of the world's most expensive woods are crafted into furniture

For nearly 150 years Knysna thrived as a port as sailing vessels, and later coastal steamers, loaded timber from the dense forests. The first attempt to establish its viability as a harbour met with disaster when, in 1817, the transport brig *Emu* was wrecked while attempting the first crossing of the bar. But later efforts were successful and it was not until the 1950s that – under the pressure of cheaper rail transport – the port was closed, leaving the lagoon to smaller craft (**192**).

Vast forestry plantations (**191**) still cover the hills surrounding the lagoon. Nor has the haven totally severed its links

191△   192▽

with maritime adventure. A thriving boat-yard here has built several internationally-renowned yachts, continuing an industry started by George Rex in 1830 when he built the first of Knysna's seagoing vessels. Rex, reputedly the son of George III from his morganatic marriage, was banished to the Cape. In 1804 he was granted the farm Melkhoutskraal, on which Knysna was to develop, and lived there for 35 years until his death. He is, in fact, better remembered than his putative father, after whom the nearby inland town of George was named. It is on the road to George that the church of Belvidere (**190**) stands – referred to as Rex's church, but built after his death.

193△   194▽

Beyond the ancient forests there is a softening of the land along the Garden Route, and a chain of lakes punctuates the littoral, separated from the sea by low brush-covered hills. Along this stretch, woody dells and reed-whispering waters vie with sparkling and seemingly endless beaches, such as that of the Wilderness (**193**). Shallow reefs sometimes fringe the headlands and are exposed at low tide, providing a bounty of oysters and other shell-fish. Survivors of an early shipwreck on this stretch of coast recorded that they 'subsisted on a diet of oysters and rainwater for nigh six weeks' as they followed the shore westwards to reach the Cape.

195△

Though none would envy the castaways their ordeal, many might covet their menu – oysters harvested from the waters between Knysna and Mossel Bay have a justified reputation as the finest and sweetest in South Africa. But pollution and over-exploitation have devastated many of the original oyster-beds and these gourmet delicacies were becoming increasingly hard to obtain when, in 1950, private enterprise and officialdom – in the shape of the Fisheries Development Corporation – stepped onto the stage.

Not far from the picturesque row of cottages which marks the entrance to Knysna (**194**), commercial oyster-beds were established. These today supply the tables of restaurants and hotels throughout the country; shipped live and still sold commercially by the gross – in spite of South Africa's metrication system – many even find their way to the sea-water tanks of hotels in other coastal resorts.

All along South Africa's coastline the sea offers up its riches, but there are others of which she appears miserly. One such treasure, until recently, was oil – a mineral which many geologists believed was present in economically workable quantities along the southern continental shelf, and one which the country's otherwise ore-rich treasure house has lacked (although South Africa did develop the world's first major viable oil-from-coal plant and remains the leader in this field).

To initiate and co-ordinate the search for the missing mineral, Soekor (the Southern Oil Exploration Corporation) was established in 1965 and funded to the tune of billions by a central government acutely conscious of the international sanctions threat. During the early 1980s encouraging traces of oil and natural gas were discovered by the giant offshore drilling rig (**195**) in the seabed off Mossel Bay. Mossgas, the operating company, went into full production in the early 1990s.

196△ 197△ 198▽ 201▷

199△ 200▽

Isolated from the mainland by 50 km or more of turbulent seas, the crews of the oil-rig off Mossel Bay have none of the communications problems of the first visitors to this stretch of coast. A regular helicopter service keeps them supplied with up-to-date entertainment, newspapers and mail. Fittingly, this private postal method based on sophisticated technology sets off from Mossel Bay (**197**); for it was here that South Africa's first postal system – based on simple ingenuity – had its beginnings.

In May 1501, Pedro d'Ataide, the captain of a small Portuguese ship not much larger than the sea-going fishing boats still built here today (**196**), put in to

Mossel Bay for fresh water. In a milkwood tree beside the spring where his crew filled their casks, he hung a sea-boot containing a letter addressed to his home. Remarkably, the letter was found less than two months later and eventually reached its destination. D'Ataide's ingenuity was commemorated by the proclamation of the milkwood as a national monument in 1938. The 'Post Office Tree' proved the precursor of what developed into a systematic, if irregular, postal service with engraved stones replacing the sea-boot as 'letter-boxes.'

Today Mossel Bay is a typical coastal town, lifted from mediocrity by the oil terminal and tank farm of its port and linked to the outside world by a modern airport as well as rail and road. Steel and concrete bridges span gorges such as that of the nearby Gouritz River (**199**) permitting a passage in seconds where progress once took days. But small boats still put to sea from here, and small boys still impatiently await the day that they will join their fathers on the fishing grounds (**201**).

It was to take more than three centuries before the seed planted by D'Ataide at Mossel Bay was to bear fruit inland. A small post office was established in Cape Town in 1792 to handle items between the settlement, Europe and the East Indies, but Hottentot runners carried official despatches to distant outposts. It was not until 1805 that regular mails began.

Post was delivered to the Drostdy – which served as both home and office of the local magistrate, or *landdrost* – and was collected from there by inhabitants of the district. But the Drostdy – that at Swellendam (**198**) is a particulary fine example of Cape Dutch architecture – was much more than a mere postal depot or even courthouse; it was the administrative centre, records repository and tax-collection office for vast tracts of territory. It was the focal point, too, of what little cultural life there was, so that it is appropriate that most Drostdys which remain today are museums – custodians of the treasures of the past (**200**) as once they were of taxes ●

202 △

203 △

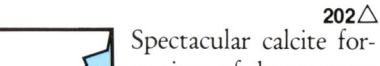

Spectacular calcite formations of almost every known type stretch in a wonderland labyrinth of colour through the limestone strata beneath the Swartberg range. These are the Cango Caves and their full extent can only be guessed. Some 2,4 km of underground passages linking 28 chambers are open to the public, but speleologists exploring the maze of the Cango Caves system have discovered several other cavern chains – at least two of which are as large as Cango – and they believe that many more exist.

Subterranean water action over tens of thousands of years first scoured the honeycomb of chambers and passages. Then, in a gentler process, it carried the soluble calcium carbonate through tiny cracks and fissures to allow the formation of stalactites and the gradual build-up from the floor beneath them of stalagmites. Throughout the chambers of the Cango network, many of these have ultimately joined to form imposing pillars (**202**), while elsewhere brilliantly coloured flowstone walls and curtains of calcite reflect the lights of visitors' headlamps (**204**). Rimstone pools, calcite flowers and straws, and helictites – which grow in all directions – add to the magic.

The caves were 'discovered' in 1780 by a farmer Van Zijl. Legend has it that one of his herders was searching for missing livestock when he stumbled on the entrance, later leading his employer there. His find is commemorated in the name 'Van Zijl's Hall' given to the largest of the chambers in the first series of caves. Here a battery of electric lights dispel the blackness to reveal a range of formations, at once grotesque and beautiful, which occupy a cavern some 100 m long and 50 m at its widest. Even larger is the 'Wonder Cave', a splendid 270 m extension of the first system and discovered in 1972. Three years after this find, another sequence of chambers 1,6 km long was probed for the first time. Dubbed 'Cango Three', its extremely difficult access and

potentially dangerous passages have prevented its opening to the public. However, speleologists (**203**) continue to explore its marvels.

Soon after Van Zijl's find, the Cape authorities claimed control of the caves, realizing even then, the probable attractions of this natural wonder – in spite of the fact that the 'visitors' of two centuries ago could not probe far, and tallow candles and weak lanterns served as their only illumination. An entrance fee was charged, trespassers were fined – though the inaccessibility of the caves must have made such transgression hard to prove or monitor – and the income 'devoted to educational purposes'.

But the late 18th-century explorers were not the true discoverers of the Cango Caves. Bushmen paintings near the main entrance indicate that it had been occupied by them. Stone artefacts – unlike those used by the Bushmen – found in the cave itself, show that their forebears lived there nearly 25 000 years ago, in the Middle Stone Age. Another life form – bats – appears to have made its home in the dark caverns from earliest times. The bat population has diminished, but at the rear of one of the chambers, groups of Cape horseshoe bats sheathed in transparent calcite indicate that they were once present in substantial numbers.

205△ 206▽

Today rivalling the nearby Cango Caves as a tourist attraction, Oudtshoorn's ostrich farms (**205, 207**) bear mute testimony to a more gracious world than that of the 1990s – a world of bustles, plumed bonnets and feather boas, a world before the widespread advent of the internal combustion engine. For it was the motor car which signalled the end of the ostrich feather boom, in whose final decade – from 1903 to 1913 – the wing and tail plumes of the world's largest bird earned South Africa almost as much as wool.

Indigenous to the continent and found throughout the drier parts of South Africa, the ostrich compensates for its inability to fly with prodigiously power-ful legs that can carry it at speeds of up to 40 km/h and can deliver a lethal kick – a combination that allows it to evade most predators. Records show that ostrich riding was a youthful pastime among early settlers – and it still provides a source of hilarity for visitors to a modern ostrich farm (**206**). But the bird's flesh was not particularly appetizing – usually there was tastier meat to be obtained from one of the many species of antelope – so that the ostrich was little hunted by the settlers.

Its eggs were, and still are, considered something of a delicacy. One ostrich egg contains the equivalent of two dozen hen's eggs, but they were not always easy

207△ 208▽ 209▽

to find. The flecked brown feathers of the female provide splendid camouflage against the dry scrub of the veld during the day, when the hen sits on her clutch of 16 or more eggs. The black plumage of the male is an ideal night-time cloak when the cock takes over the role of incubation and guarding the nest.

The indigenous Bushmen used ostrich egg shells to carry and to cache water. They also ground pieces of the thick, durable shell into disc-like beads thousands of years before the coming of the white settlers. These beads were not only popular adornment among the Bushmen but were also extensively used by the black Bantu-speaking tribes. The latter included ostrich feathers as part of their ceremonial regalia.

But until the 1860s the ostrich went largely undisturbed – inflating his neck when angered (208), taking to his heels when threatened, and subsisting on the meagre peckings of the veld. Then a sudden change in fashion in distant Europe gave the ostrich unexpected economic importance. Almost overnight the long plumes became an essential accessory in the milliner's craft, while the lesser wing feathers, or 'spadonas', were in great demand for feather boas.

To the farmer of the Little Karoo, scratching from the land an existence almost as mean as that of the ostrich, the new vogue for feathers was a godsend. His stock was freely available in the veld and, provided he could catch a pair of ostriches, his only capital outlay was to fence a paddock and sow lucerne. The ostriches, their large clutches of eggs now protected from predators, bred more prolifically than they had done in the wild. Wing feathers could be plucked every six months or so. By 1900 some 750 000 of the birds were 'farmed', but demand continued to outstrip supply and prices rose accordingly. The new wealth was reflected in a rash of ornate buildings (209) and the ostrich farmer rode high, until the vogue for feathers was blown away in the slipstream of the motor car.

◁**210** **211**△ **212**▽

To the farmer of the Little Karoo both his land and the weather are animate; the earth is masculine, taciturn and reliable – though not always benevolent – while the elements are feminine, temperamental and unpredictable. It is a chauvinism of the mid-18th Century, understandable in a people whose attitudes have little changed since their forebears came to this harsh stretch of veld and koppies (**211**). Such towns as Ladismith and Oudtshoorn did enjoy brief impetus towards progress and prosperity given by the ostrich boom. But, though these towns fall within the area between the Langeberg and Swartberg ranges which geographers define as the Little Karoo, they are not truly of it.

The true Little Karoo knows no geographical limits. Rather it is a state of mind, often anachronistic in the 20th-Century world, ruggedly masculine in its individuality, often eccentric in its expression. And because it is foremost a state of mind and only secondly a region, it is appropriate that the most typically

Little Karoo town is many kilometres beyond the Swartberg mountains. Aberdeen, where carefully-tended beds of Namaqualand daisies and other ephemerals blaze along the fringes of its main street (**210**), for many years boasted the highest church steeple in southern Africa. But because it was built in the spirit of the Little Karoo, the spire is glaringly unperpendicular.

In the Little Karoo money is still frequently banked in tin chests tucked under the farmer's four-poster bed. Occasional Post Offices are farmhouse kitchens, where outgoing letters and parcels share the shelves with jars of preserved fruit, and stamps are sold from a tea caddy. The actual mail is as often as not collected from the nearest dorp or distant railway siding by donkey cart (**212**) at the convenience of the farmer/post master.

Sometimes individual idiosyncracies stand out, even in this eccentric land. Until recently a Bellair Dam farmer – one of the few in his community who had partly bowed to the trappings of the present century – drove his sheep to the market town of

213▽

215▽

214▽

Barrydale in a pre-war Rolls Royce, his wife and brood of children crammed with him on the chauffeur's bench. Even in the 'Looking Glass' world of the Little Karoo eyebrows were raised – until he explained that the sliding glass window, which had once ensured privacy for stately passengers, protected his neck from the sheep's moist noses, and diminished the pungent smell. In this land of pepper trees and thornbush, where in the driest regions men still move their flocks across several hundred kilometres of bare veld in search of richer pasturage (**215**), it was a simple logic which his peers could understand.

And when the rainbow's promise is made good, and she rejuvenates the land, the farmer will make his way to the church in the dorp (**213**) to give thanks to a God whom he knows with utter certainty is masculine. And as the land dries out again, the presence of water again marked only by the stands of gum trees which denote each farm or wayside resting place (**214**), he will survey his taciturn fields and know life to be good.

216△ 217▽

Rising from the coastal plains of the southern Cape in a dignified splendour of golden buttresses and purple-shadowed kloofs, the Swartberg range marks an abrupt transition from rain-blessed arable lands where fields of wheat and lucerne lie rich in the sun (**216**) to the apparent poverty of the semi-desert Karoo. Yet this harsh hinterland, which comprises one-third of South Africa's surface, has a richness of its own; its very aridity has led to the evolution of a unique vegetation, impressive in its variety and fascinating in its tenacity.

Broken only by flat-topped dolomite koppies, or infrequently riven by grotesquely-eroded kloofs, the Karoo's brown sameness conceals a world of succulents and desert ephemerals. Euphorbias, stapelias, aloes and mesembryanthemums, whose fleshy leaves and roots allow them to store moisture, are found in an abundance of differing species. Many ephemerals, whose seeds lie dormant between the rains – sometimes several arid years apart – germinate and grow rapidly when kissed by the

first shower, and briefly carpet the veld in rainbow colours before casting their seeds to await the next moist blessing. A great number of these plants have been exported and form the nuclei of 'desert gardens' in Europe and the Americas, while Japanese plant breeders have developed the humble, indigenous lithops, or stone plant, into a multi-hued range of vegetation more like jewels than the pebbles which the originals mimic.

There is also a rugged, albeit savage, beauty in the infrequent basalt outcrops which dot the Karoo landscape. Oases of misshapen rocks – such as the 30 and 40 m-high pinnacles of the Valley of Desolation (**217**) – break the monotony of the landscape as if to emphasize its inhospitality. It is an inhospitality emphasized by the steady decline in numbers of its inhabitants; of all South Africa, only in the Karoo does the population continue to diminish. Yet even in such isolated spots, man's flocks find food, and the strumming of a *veewagter's* home-made guitar (**218**) is sometimes heard ●

The sense of empty desolation of much of Africa's hinterland is echoed on the stretch of coast that points to the continent's southernmost tip and the Agulhas light which is its final punctuation (**221**). Long centuries before the white man came, clans of *Strandlopers*, Stone-Age beach-combers, grubbed a meagre existence along this shore, living on shell-fish and other marine life. Their presence is attested to by frequent shell middens – their kitchen rubbish dumps, from which the modern archaeologist can piece together details of the daily life of these early inhabitants. Tidal fish-traps which

221△ 222▽

the *Strandlopers* constructed are still used today, not far from the coastal village of Waenhuiskrans where the quiet of picturesque fishermen's cottages with their reed-thatched roofs (**219**) belies the rigorous existence of their occupants.

The sea here is never completely at ease. Swift tides and treacherous currents make the coloured fisherman's life a hard one, and the waters of this coast have taken their tribute of many lives. It was near Waenhuiskrans – so named for the enormous sea-cave, accessible only at low tide (**222**), which early farmers likened to a giant coach-house – that the East Indiaman *Arniston* was wrecked in 1815 with the loss of 372 lives. And it was as Arniston, in the 1930s, that an enterprising property agent promoted the sale of beachfront cottages. But it is as Waenhuiskrans that its fisherfolk still know it, their working presence as much a reminder as the old harbour at nearby Hermanus (**220**), that most Cape coastal resorts had their beginnings in the harvest of the seas ●

223△ 224▽

To early mariners, beating against the winds and currents to pass its threatening rocks, it was the 'Cape of Storms'. And while Sir Francis Drake, on his epic of circumnavigation wrote of it as 'the most stately thing, and the fairest Cape we saw in the whole circumference of the earth', the southern tip of the Cape Peninsula creates an awesome pattern of wave-wracked sea (**223**). Its waters are turbulent, the meeting-place of the warm Agulhas Current and the cold Benguela in a clash of temperature that on windless days can create sudden dense fog that blankets the upper sections of the 250 m

sandstone cliffs of Cape Point, yet leaves the lower-lying Cape of Good Hope (**225**) uncovered.

In 1911, the ill-fated liner *Lusitania* was wrecked off Cape Point when the lonely warning beacon was hidden by such a fog covering the summit of Vasco da Gama Peak – then the site of the lighthouse. The disaster led to the present lighthouse being built lower down the point – probably a boon to the men who attend it, for the peak above is recognized as the windiest spot in South Africa, not only in terms of wind frequency but of its velocity as well.

And when the gales blow here, howling across the rocky outcrops and *fynbos*

scrubland of the Cape Point Nature Reserve, one can sense the forces (**224**) which created the legend of the Flying Dutchman. It was to round this Cape that Van der Decken, unable to make headway against the rage of a south-easterly storm, defied the Almighty to stop him doing so

– only to find himself and his ship condemned to roam the sea for ever, day and night, 'until the trump of God shall rend the sky'.

Two centuries before Van der Decken is supposed to have left Holland with his swashbuckling crew *en route* to Batavia in search of a fortune, the Portuguese navigator Bartolomeu Dias was spared a similar elemental battle when his small flotilla was blown hundreds of kilometres off course and became the first to round the Cape, without seeing it or realizing that they had done so. He rectified this on his return voyage and landed at Cape Maclear to erect a cross or *padrão*, a replica of which stands there today (**226**).

227△ 228▽ 229▽

Though more than 30 years separated their activities, a down-to-earth German and *joie de vivre* Frenchman – one with an eye to the commercial possibilities of dried salt fish, the other with a gourmet's appreciation of rock lobster – effectively fathered South Africa's fishing industry and, in so doing, changed the face of Hout Bay.

Fish had been caught for local consumption from the first days of white settlement – and by the indigenous peoples for many hundreds of years before that. But it was not until 1867 that an immigrant farmer in the Hout Bay valley, Jacob Trautmann, decided that the shoals of snoek which teem off the Peninsula's Atlantic coastline in autumn and early winter could be harvested, salted and dried. It was a process which his Baltic ancestors had perfected generations previously. The snoek – a large mackerel-like fish with a powerful predatory jaw – tends to deteriorate more quickly than the European species with which Trautmann was familiar. However, he devised a way of

preserving it, and he found a ready market for his product among the protein-hungry workers of the sugar plantations of Mauritius. An export industry, which a century later was to see South Africa in the 'Top Ten' of the world's fishing nations, was born.

Snoek are still landed and processed at Hout Bay, although smoking has replaced Trautmann's methods, to create a favoured delicacy from this fish rather than a labourer's diet. Today Hout Bay's fishing fleet (**227**) harvests other food from the sea as well. An even greater delicacy today is rock lobster. Some still remember when this, too, was part of the working man's daily fare and a large bag of the succulent claws and legs could be bought for a penny.

Here it was the gourmet Frenchman Lucien Plessis who realized the potential. In 1903 he bought the hull of a British barque, the *R. Morrow,* which had been wrecked off Mouille Point. He had it towed to Hout Bay and turned it into a

230▽   231▽

canning factory to process rock lobster which he exported to France. A mysterious explosion in 1914 tore the factory apart, killing M. Plessis and seven of his employees. But the fish-canning industry which he began still flourishes, and rock lobster tails processed at Hout Bay are exported to almost every segment of the globe.

The international fishing boom of the post-war years gave the fishing harbour (**228**) a fillip. Substantial accommodation for the coloured fishermen (**229**) and their families was built as the dockside factory and processing plants expanded – much to the annoyance of the beach-front residents and inhabitants of the largely rural valley extending beyond the dunes. It is a controversy which erupts sporadically as conservationists and industry continue an irreconcilable verbal battle.

Conservation was also far from the thoughts of the first white settlers to visit the valley. Within a month of Van Riebeeck's arrival in April 1652, his men had discovered that the

valley contained many fine tall trees. A rough road was hastily built over Constantia Nek and timber was felled. Even then the needs of progress were the first to be served. In fact the only recorded visitors to Hout Bay who left it virtually untouched appear to have been the crew of *H.M.S. Consent*. They paused here in 1607 after sailing under the looming cliffs of Hangberg and the Sentinel to the anchorage, today guarded by a mediocre sculpture of a bronze leopard (**231**). They came briefly ashore – the Mate John Chapman was accidentally almost left behind – and then sailed on, the only sign of their visit, the words 'Chapman's Chance' marked on a chart. Today the lucky sailor is remembered in the name given to Chapman's Peak and its scenic drive (**230**) which rivals the Mediterranean Corniche for spectacle. In places sliced out of vertical rock, the road curves and winds a breath-taking route from Hout Bay to the unbroken sweep of Noordhoek's unspoilt beach where small-boat fishermen put out to catch rock lobster.

232△ 233▽   234▽ 235▽

When the first colonists arrived in Table Bay to establish a provision station, they came to a land already rich in flora. It took them some time, however, to realize the wealth of edible plants awaiting them and they paid scant, if any, attention to the even greater treasure-house of unique vegetation which the land encompassed. And it was a botanical treasure-house; South Africa's floral kingdom is the richest in the world, with more than 18 500 indigenous flowering species alone. The *fynbos* of the Table Mountain range, in whose shadow Van Riebeeck and his tiny garrison had settled, comprises more than 2 500 forms of plant – the greatest range in Nature found so compactly.

But the settlers, whose first attempts at cultivation had failed, were more concerned with food than flora, with bread than botany. They were forced to experiment with *veldkos* – roots, herbs and the fruits of indigenous plants such as oxalis, or sorrel, and the young shoots of palmiet to provide 'greens' for their diet. This was the limit of their interest. Faced as they were with carving out a new land, their pre-occupation with the utilitarian is understandable.

Yet all around them grew some of the world's most intriguing flora including the cycads (**232**), unchanged representatives of plants which flourished between 200 and 300 million years ago,

6△   **237**▽   **238**▽   **239**▽

before any flowering species inhabited the earth. Two genera – *Stangeria* and *Encephalartos* – are found only in South Africa. Full realization of the extent of the Cape's botanical wealth did not come about for nearly 100 years. Then, with the arrival of such skilled scientists as Masson and Thunberg, the riches were disclosed to an astonished and fascinated Europe whose botanical gardens were inundated with specimens and seeds.

There, courtier-botanists vied with each other to grow such 'exotics' as the protea, with the bearded protea (**233**), pincushions (**238**) and *suikerbos,* South Africa's best-loved species (**236**), proving particularly popular.

The seeds of the Kafferboom, or common erythrina (**235**) which are a deep red with a black spot, soon became as popular as 'lucky beads' in Europe as they were among the indigenous peoples, while the sometimes grotesque flower-heads of other members of the protea family (**234**) so closely resembled those found in Australia that botanists were baffled. Only many years later did the theory of Gondwanaland and a vast continental split, provide a plausible explanation. Today many of these 'exotics' are grown throughout the world and a strelitzia (**237**) is as likely to be found in Stockholm as an everlasting (**239**) in Edgebaston.

Even the aggressive façade of concrete high-rise buildings and the serpentine curves of pillar-borne freeways cannot hide the charm of Cape Town. South Africa's second largest and mother city enjoys perhaps the loveliest setting of any metropolis in the world, even though high-rise development now clothes the gently sloping shore where Jan van Riebeeck and his small party landed in April 1652, to establish a victualling station for Dutch East Indian Company ships en route to the spice islands of the Orient. A labyrinth of offices rises on land reclaimed from the sea

240△　　　241▽

where his flagship, the *Drommedaris,* rode at anchor; and a vast container terminal stretches from the beach where an earlier mariner, Antonio de Saldanha, landed in 1501.

To Saldanha is attributed the honour of being the first white person to climb Table Mountain (**240**), whose

eroded sandstone grandeur dominates the city – a grandeur heightened at night during the summer months, when its precipitous northern face is floodlit (**244**). The lower slopes are now denuded of the woody thickets through which the first European colonists forced their way. Most of the trees that grace the area are in plantations of imported pines and eucalyptus.

The changes, begun by Van Riebeeck, have been gradual. His brief from the *Here XVII* – the Council of Seventeen in Holland – was practical. He was to establish a fort and a company garden; to accrue enough livestock from

242△   243▽

244▽

the indigenous Hottentot herders to supply the Company's passing ships with sufficient meat to keep the crews contented; and to provide enough fresh vegetables to keep them free of scurvy.

Initially, barter with the Hottentots proved easy, but Van Riebeeck's first attempts at cultivation were anything but successful. Winds not only leached the topsoil, but blew seeds and seedlings away. The few straggly vegetables and corn which survived this onslaught were scorched by sun and the salt-laden air. Nevertheless, the Company gardener Hendrick Hendricx Boom managed to salvage enough seed from the battered crops to ensure a second planting. This time the settlers were more successful. Fruit trees from St Helena were cultivated and, as more land came under the plough, vines were imported from Europe. Both these introductions were to prove the first steps in developing South Africa's agricultural economy.

But if cultivation of crops was beginning to thrive, cultivation of good-neighbourliness with the indigenous population was not. Armed skirmishes with the Hottentots – who had grazed and hunted the lands where Cape Town's suburbs now sprawl (**241**) – grew increasingly frequent. A chain of forts, ancillary to the 'castle', were thrown up along the Liesbeek River – then reed-fringed and the habitat of hippo, but today a concrete-sided canal.

Now rivalling the mountain as the city's premier tourist attraction is the Victoria and Alfred Waterfront (**242** and **243**), a newly converted part of Cape Town's historic harbour offering a lively melange of dockside entertainment.

◁245   247△   248▽

246▽

Today tall blocks of beachfront flats resist the winds which wreaked such havoc with Hendrick Boom's first attempts at cultivation, for it was at Sea Point, under the slopes of Signal Hill, that he sowed his ill-fated fields of corn. To the seafront lawn and the immense sea-water pool (**245**) that are features of this cosmopolitan suburb, the youth of Cape Town flock day in and day out. In high summer it becomes a mecca for a myriad holiday-makers, its restaurant-filled main street thronging with hungry visitors. But even here there is something of the *grande dame*, for the pleasures of Sea Point seem more sedate than those of Durban's frenetic Golden Mile.

249 ▽   250 ▷

And, despite the modern glass and glitter of the Foreshore, where Jan van Riebeeck's statue peers towards the mountain through the spray of playing fountains (**246**), the Mother City *is* sedate. In the eyes of Capetonians her serenity confirms that 'everything is for the best in this best of all possible worlds'. Strolling down Government Avenue of oaks where Boom eventually established his vegetable garden, and past the mellow buildings which house the Republic's parliament (**247**), the visitor may forgive the dowager such smugness. She retains a dignity suited to a life that has seen the tiny first settlement grow from sod and timber to stones and bricks

and mortar. She has experienced the changes from the days of Company control, through colonial administration to self-government; and for part of each year she is the home of the country's politicians when parliament meets.

Cape Town's buildings, as much as her air of history, contribute to the proud stateliness which mantles much of the city's centre. Though sleek cars swish across the cobbles of Greenmarket Square with its Old Town House (**248**), the clop of horses and a trundling carriage passing its steps seems more appropriate. The Victorian splendour of the city hall presides over the flower-sellers on the Grand Parade (**250**), yet even here the

idiosyncracies of the dowager are apparent. The clock in its central tower – once as punctual as the noonday gun still fired each day from the battery on the slopes of Signal Hill – in recent years has kept, more often than not, a time of its own.

The Grand Parade has seen almost as much of the city's history as has the mountain. Now separated from the sea by railway marshalling yards and a plethora of roads and buildings, it was once part of the great bay's shoreline and was scoured by the cleansing south-east winds – the Cape Doctor. In winter the 'Doctor' rests and a blanket of fog (**249**) often lies over the Cape Flats which link the Peninsula with the rest of Africa.

251△ 252▽ 253▽

Cape Town, today's serenely-poised dowager, was once a seaman's moll. Although the settlement on the shores of Table Bay had its origins as a garden, it was as a port that it reached maturity and earned the name 'Tavern of the Seas'. For the bay was actually an ideal summer anchorage and was used regularly by passing ships after De Saldanha's discovery. But even in the summer months the sea could throw up a sudden vicious storm such as that expierenced in 1647, when the Dutch *Nieuwe Haerlem* foundered on a sandbank near modern Milnerton. Some of the *Nieuwe Haerlem's* crew spent more than a year ashore protecting her valuable cargo. Though

254△ 255▽

their temporary settlement did not influence the Council of Seventeen's decision to establish a way-station at the Cape, their experience proved valuable in planning a permanent maritime outpost

By the time the small colony was established and the first Free Burgher farmers had begun to cultivate the land in earnest, ships of all the world's maritime nations were making use of Table Bay. In the grog shops and taverns of the waterfront, Spanish reals, English pounds and French louis were as acceptable as the Dutch gulden. Table Bay was at times a forest of masts and spars and some 50 ships were anchored here when during a severe storm in 1722, 11 British and

Dutch ships were wrecked. However, maritime activity, which continues today (**251**), reached its peak in the 1950s and 1960s when the closure of the Suez Canal returned the Cape to its role as a haven for the ships of all nations.

There is no record of how long it took De Saldanha and his fellow mariners to climb what he named *Taboa de Cabo* or 'Table Cape', though he probably followed the steep but easy route up the Platteklip Gorge which gashes the mountain face above the city. The aerial cableway (**252**) which began operation in 1929 whisks the modern visitor to the plateau summit in a matter of minutes. A viewing area near the upper cable station

provides a spectacular vista of the Peninsula, including the immense sweep of Table Bay (**253**), with its western bastion of Lion's Head and its Rump – now known as Signal Hill.

Where Table Mountain's summit provides superb views of the bay and the city, Rhodes Memorial (**254**) on the lower, south-eastern slopes of Devil's Peak is an equally fine vantage-point from which to view the sprawl of development creeping across the Cape Flats towards the distant Hottentots Holland mountains. Near by is the Groote Schuur estate, Rhodes' home (**255**) which served for many years as the Prime Minister's official residence.

256△   257▽   259▽

On its Atlantic side the rocky spine of the Cape Peninsula plunges steeply to the sea. Here the sheer face of the mountain is cut by a spectacular series of kloofs and ravines into a chain of buttresses which Van Riebeeck described as the *Gewelbergen* (or Gable Mountains). Today they are known as the Twelve Apostles (**256**) – something of a misnomer, as 18 of the outcrops guard the mountain's flank before it dips to the gentle curve of Hout Bay. Nestling at their feet are some of the Cape's most popular beaches, where – perhaps because the water is colder than that of False Bay – the youthful and the no-longer-so-youthful come to see and be seen rather than to swin. These are the bikini beaches of Clifton and Camps Bay (**257**) where the sun sets late and a tan is more important than the state of the surf or the temperature of the water.

The beaches of False Bay are arguably finer, and Kipling maintained that 'the white sands of Muizenberg' which 'marched silver to the sea' were the finest in the world. Poetic

258△ **260△** **261▽**

licence perhaps, but there are many who would agree with him. Muizenberg, though it is often whipped by the summer's prevalent south-easterly winds, was the Peninsula's most popular resort, drawing thousands of inland holidaymakers. And though many of its hotels have closed, its 'snake pit' – where oiled bodies bask in profusion – still exerts its powerful attraction. The long sweep of Sunrise Beach with its attendant lines of bathing boxes (**259**) offers a sense of unmatched space and freedom. Here, too, a surfer finds freedom of a different sort as he rides the steep slope of a breaking wave as it rolls towards the beach (**258**) while a fishing boat passes unconcerned on its return to the nearby harbour of Kalk Bay. And in the lonely moments waiting for the swell to rise (**260**), he may hear the lowing of ghostly cattle, for Muizenberg had its origins in 1673 as a humble cattle post whose herdsman's house – recently restored – is said to be second only to the Castle as the Republic's oldest extant building.

Muizenberg was transformed in status to an important military outpost when Simon's Bay became the official winter anchorage of the Dutch East India Company's fleet. In 1795, it echoed to the sound of cannon and musket-fire when troops landed here and defeated the Dutch garrison in what proved to be the decisive battle leading to the first British occupation of the Cape and the end of the Company's control.

At nearby Fish Hoek (**261**) a battle of a different sort continues to this day, as proponents and opponents of an historic ban on liquor argue whether or not the resort should remain 'dry' – the only teetotal municipality in South Africa. The ban dates from 1818 when Lord Charles Somerset granted the 1 117 ha on which the town stands to a farmer, Andries Bruins, on condition that the right of fishing should remain free and that no public wine-house should be opened. Along the beach fishermen still ply their trek-nets without hinderance – and a plethora of clubs testify to Fish Hoek's 'aridity'.

Lord Charles Somerset's gubernatorial ban on wine sales extended no further than Fish Hoek, but there may well have been times when he wished that it did. When he took office in 1814 the flourishing wine industry was in disarray, the once-high reputation of Cape wines had fallen to a nadir, and attempts by his predecessor to stop the rot by appointing an official taster for export wines had failed. Lord Charles was no more successful. Cape wines continued to be exported to Britain at a rate of some three million litres a year, but they were considered suitable only for cheap blending.

The situation which the Governor inherited stemmed directly from the

264△　265▽　266▽

Napoleonic wars and Whitehall's decision to turn the Cape into her private wine-cellar. Britain encouraged production by a series of tariff preferences which back-fired when the wine farmers of the western Cape opted for quick, handsome profits at the cost of quality.

Today Cape wines have regained their erstwhile high reputation and are exported throughout the free world. Their quality has been strictly controlled by the K.W.V. whose cellars at Paarl house the world's largest maturing casks (**264**).

Soon after his arrival, Van Riebeeck urged the authorities in Holland to supply him with vines, arguing that they should be as successful on the local hillsides as they were on those of France and Spain. But it was not until three years later, in 1655, that the first vines arrived and almost four years after that – in February 1659 – that he recorded: 'Today, praise be to God, wine was made for the first time from Cape grapes . . .'

The early success of these official oenological efforts encouraged the Free Burghers to follow suit. By the time that Simon van der Stel retired to his homestead Groote Constantia (**263**), in whose cellars (**262**) wine is still produced, more than 400 000 vines had been planted. But wine-making was not part of the Dutch agricultural tradition and the early wines were of poor quality. It was not until 1688 and the arrival of the French Huguenots, who brought with them wine-making expertise, that production went from strength to strength and the reputation of 'Constantia' grew.

Whether that reputation would ever have recovered from the mediocrity of the early 19th Century but for the devastation of *Phylloxera* is moot. When this virus attacked the local vineyards in 1886, exports of the inferior product were booming. But, in a matter of months, the vines were almost exterminated and the old wine-presses (**265**) fell silent. Recovery, with virus-resistant stocks, was slow, encouraging a return to quality in today's harvest (**266**).

Of the French Protestant refugees who fled their homeland to England and Holland following the revocation of the Edict of Nantes, a mere 200 made their way to the Cape in 1688-89. But this handful was to have a disproportionate impact on South Africa's development; not only did the Huguenots give impetus to the young wine industry, but they brought with them an invigorating culture which the Dutch and German burghers lacked. The Free Burghers, former Dutch East India Company employees who were granted land after a contractual period of service, were mainly of poor, peasant stock and had little of the newcomers' refinement. At the Cape

269△ 270▽

271▽

the Huguenots were allowed their own church council and minister of religion, but they were not permitted to form a separate community. Instead they were intermingled among the existing Boland farms in the Drakenstein area and the fertile Franschhoek valley, where a striking monument (**267**) commemorates their contribution to the land's development.

The growing wealth of the Cape farmers, to which the Huguenots' skills contributed, found visible expression in a unique form of architecture – the Cape Dutch style, characterized by soaring gables. Though these gables owed something to those of the high narrow townhouses of Holland, in the open

spaces of the African landscape they evolved a grace of their own. Their uniquely fine proportion can be appreciated in the solitary splendour of a rural manor-house (**271**) as readily as in the streets of a growing town. Those of Tulbagh (**268**), restored to their original glory after the town was devastated by an earthquake in the late 1960s, are a perfect example. Their interiors, typified by the furnishings in Paarl's Pastorie Museum (**270**) echo both the grace of this style of building and the new found wealth of those farmers. More functional but also elegant in its simple lines is the VOC Kruithuis, or powder magazine, built on Stellenbosch's De Braak in 1777.

272 △   275 ▷

273 △   274 ▽

Time has marked a myriad changes throughout the Boland as elsewhere in South Africa, but there are pockets along the country's bleak west coast where, if the clock has not stopped, it has at least slowed down. Where the small fishing villages and hamlets follow a pattern of existence which has little changed in the past 100 years and a donkey cart (272) trundling past an old church with its attendant bell-towers is not yet an anachronism. On the fringes of the bay, small boats still line the beach above high-water (275). Their owners' reed-thatched cottages have changed no more than have their fishing methods, while at Churchhaven at the further end of the Langebaan Lagoon where the receding tides leave the salt-flats bare (274), life-styles have deteriorated.

A once-thriving community of coloured fisherfolk and their white cousins, the three hamlets which comprise Churchhaven linger on only to accommodate their aged. Diminishing in-shore

catches and the closure of the nearby Donkergat whaling station, formerly a source of employment for both men and women, reduced the inhabitants' livelihood to subsistence and drove the young people to seek work in the town or in the larger fishing centres of the coast. Now only the areas' popularity as a weekend retreat for the rat-race-weary inhabitants of Cape Town promises a future. Other villages face a similar fate, yet the fishermen continue their calling (**276**) despite its meagre returns (**277**).

Saldanha Bay, however, has seen a recent development as the iron-ore terminal serving the inland mines at Sishen. From here almost daily, iron-ore trains – often more than a kilometre long – hurtle across the wastes of the northern Cape to discharge their cargo into the waiting holds of bulk carriers. The piers of the terminal, resting on the fossilized remains of a two-million-year-old oyster bed, provide a back-drop to the deep-sea fishing boats returning to a bustling harbour with their catches (**273**).

276▽

277▽

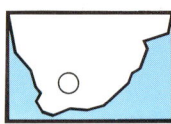Across the shimmering heat haze of the Karoo a distant beacon beckons and the dust-weary traveller licks dried lips with the same sense of relief that the early trekkers through this semi-desert must have felt when their oxen quickened their pace at the scent of water. The beacon is a church spire, mark of every town or dorp in this landscape of desolate beauty, and a welcome break in a horizon otherwise fringed only with flat-topped koppies. Nothing is visible in this arid waste to indicate that it was once the site of enormous, steaming swamps in which life developed more than 300 million years ago. Yet in its shales the Karoo holds hidden the fossil remains of aconites – among the earliest of life forms – of fish, and of mammal-like reptiles that bridged the evolutionary span between water and land. Then these parts were moist and lush; today they are semi-desert.

Technically the Karoo covers one-third of South Africa and is slowly spreading eastwards. It is marked more by its vegetation than by any geographical boundaries. The plants have a high nutritional value, but are generally so sparse that some 4 ha of veld is needed to feed each of the sheep or goats (**279**) on which the Karoo's agriculture is based. Colesberg (**278**) breaks slightly with this pattern as an important horse-breeding centre. Otherwise, with Graaff-Reinet, it best typifies the centres of Karoo farming. Colesberg was founded in the first half of the 19th Century on the site of an abandoned London Missionary Society station. Plots on the main street were sold to finance the building of the Dutch Reformed Church which dominates the town. Its early houses – many of which still stand – are a fascinating architectural combination of Cape Dutch and Georgian styles and were built with flat roofs because of the lack of suitable thatching reeds in the vicinity.

But there are man-made oases other than those marked by the beacons of church spires. Despite its arid surface drabness,

◁278   279△

280△   281▽

there is considerable underground water in the Karoo. Where man has tapped it, often boring hundreds of metres into the rocky shale to do so, the green of lawns, gardens and the ubiquitous lucerne marks a typical farmstead (**280**).

To the modern traveller, Matjiesfontein presents an oasis of a different, probably more welcome sort. This village, established as a health resort in the 1880s and today a popular hotel complex, was the first in South Africa to have water-borne sewerage. The London street lamps with which the village's founder clocked up another first – electricity – still light its only street (**281**). The turret of the Lord Milner Hotel, built during the early stages of the second Anglo-Boer War, was later used as a look-out post when the village was commandeered as the headquarters of a 12 000-strong British garrison. It was from these troops that the force intended to relieve the siege of Kimberley was drawn, only to suffer a heavy defeat at the battle of Magersfontein.

A giant crater 1 097 m deep is today the empty reminder of the discovery in 1866 of a 'pretty pebble' that was to change the course of South African history. It was not until 1870 that the first of four diamondiferous blue-ground pipes was discovered where Kimberley now stands. The 21,75-carat diamond which 15-year-old Erasmus Jacobs found on the bank of the Orange River awakened geologists and prospectors to the presence in the north-eastern Cape of the hardest and most treasured of all known crystals.

The nine-metre-high Colesberg Koppie, which was the last of the four pipes uncovered, soon disappeared under the picks and shovels of the diggers, to be-

282△　　　　　　283▽

come the Big Hole (**282**), until recently the biggest man-made crater in the world. Prospectors flocked from other claims, established in the two previous years, to the site. As the diggers delved ever deeper into the diamond-rich Kimberlite, pathways which had criss-crossed the claims disappeared and opencast mining developed. Small claims were bought out, but 14 years after the excavations started, there were still 98 operators. It was then that Cecil Rhodes and his partners began financial machinations which led to the eventual creation of De Beers Consolidated Mines, the most powerful force in the world's diamond market. When mining of the Big Hole ceased in 1914 it

284△ 285▽

had yielded more than three tonnes (14 504 375 carats) of diamonds.

Kimberley remains the centre of diamond sorting (283) and it is here, too, that the small private prospectors (285) bring their finds for valuation and sale.

Another link with the early mining days is 'Long Cecil', the field-gun which stands in the shadow of the town's war memorial (284). Designed and built at Rhodes' request during the siege of Kimberley, the gun was the creation of an American mining engineer, George Labram, and proved so successful that the Boers brought up their own 'Long Tom' in retaliation – its last shot killing Labram who was resting in his hotel.

The red-brown sands of the desert seem to stretch forever, their colours echoed by equally lonely cloudscapes as the sun drops behind the horizon of the Kalahari. It is a stark landscape where the passing of a donkey with its rider is noteworthy and the passage of two is an event (**286**). It is a land better suited to the gemsbok (**288**) than to man, a lost corner of the northern Cape which nevertheless saw the brief fruition of not one, but two ill-fated republics – Stellaland and Goshen.

Both came into being as the result of inter-tribal warfare among the Bechuana, or Tswana, who had inhabited this empty

288△ 289▽

land for centuries before the first white explorers probed north to the fabled Kingdom of Latakoo. In 1882 the pro-British Batlapin chief Mankurwane was defeated by the Korana chief David Massouw, the latter achieving victory with the armed assistance of a group of Transvaal burghers. As a reward for their aid, Massouw granted the Transvalers a tract of land reaching north and south of the Harts River. Here, in August 1883, they established the 'Republic of the Star', or Stellaland, with Vryburg as its capital. The newly-found republic adopted the constitution of the neighbouring Transvaal, designed its own flag and coat of arms and even issued its own postage stamps. It seemed set to enjoy peaceful prosperity.

Moves were begun to incorporate Stellaland with the Transvaal but, before negotiations were concluded, the London Convention of 1884 fixed the western limits of the Transvaal at the existing boundary, so that the tiny Boer enclave was forced to remain isolated.

A similar fate befell the Republic of Goshen which had been established a year earlier than Stellaland and some distance to the north. Its origins also lay in a clash of black tribes – in this instance Moswete of the Kunwana defeated a Barolong chief – the victor awarding a substantial grant of land to the Boers who had aided him. A 'capital' was established at a spot appropriately named Rooigrond, or 'red earth', and affiliation with the Transvaal Republic was sought. Both fledgling republics surrendered to a British invasion force in 1885, without bloodshed or even a shot being fired. Both of the tiny republics were incorporated into what was then the Bechuanaland Protectorate; a decade later they joined the Cape.

Possibly the burghers – isolated and without even a viable agricultural economy – were glad to see the last of the two short-lived states. Certainly the land remains little loved, its silence disturbed only by the clank of an infrequent windmill (**287**) or the bleating of a flock of goats (**289**).

290△　291▽

Sun City, set in the dun and green grasslands two hours' drive to the north of the Johannesburg-Pretoria conurbation, is southern Africa's answer to Las Vegas: a glittering and unashamedly hedonistic fun factory whose four hotels and crowded gaming rooms are designed to distract, amuse and pamper three million visitors a year. Outdoor relaxation features prominently in the scheme. Among the several sparkling swimming pools is one that embraces an island of tall Washingtonia and phoenix date palms (**290**); other, even more spectacular venues are

292△

293△   294▽

Waterworld, a 750-metre, man-made, lushly fringed lake, and the Waterscape, a sequence of three interlinked pools, 12 waterfalls and 2 km of walkways that take you through some of the most exquisite of landscaped grounds.

Focus of indoor activity is the Entertainment Centre, a busy concentration of restaurants, bars, discos, cinemas, acres of slot machines (**293**), the exuberant Extravaganza Theatre (**294**), the famed casino and the 7 000-seat Superbowl, used for conventions, international title-fights and, latterly, for the annual Miss World contest.

Pride of Sun City, though, is the recently completed Lost City development, central feature of which is the Palace hotel (**291** and **292**), a fantastic complex of domes and minarets, ultraluxurious suites, an entrance hall that rises three storeys and, in the grounds, an instant 'jungle' of beautiful trees and a 100-by-60-metre swimming pool swept by artificially created surfing waves.

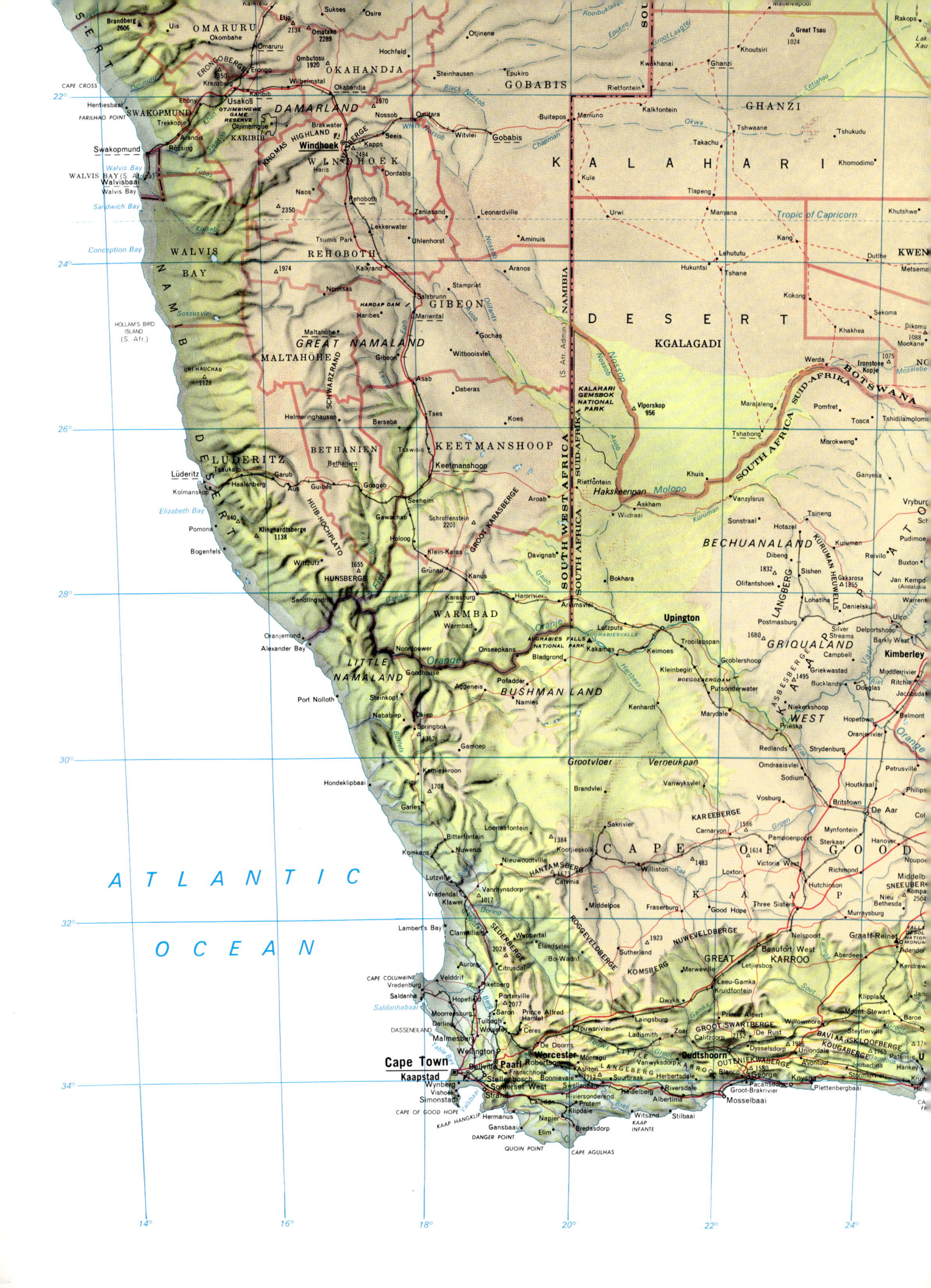

Republic of South Africa

Copyright by Rand McNally & Company, R.L.75.1-5

Scale 1:6,000,000

One centimeter represents 60 kilometers.
One inch represents approximately 95 miles.

Kilometers
Statute Miles

Meters	Feet
6000	19685
4000	13124
3000	9843
2000	6562
1000	3281
500	1640
200	656
0	0